The Children *of* Children Keep Coming

The Children *of* Children Keep Coming

an epic Griotsong

Russell L. Goings
images by Romare Bearden

POCKET BOOKS KAREN HUNTER PUBLISHING
NEW YORK LONDON TORONTO SYDNEY

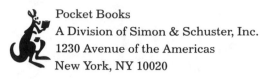

Pocket Books
A Division of Simon & Schuster, Inc.
1230 Avenue of the Americas
New York, NY 10020

Karen Hunter Publishing
A Division of Suitt-Hunter Enterprises, LLC
598 Broadway, 3rd Floor
New York, NY 10012

First Karen Hunter Publishing/Pocket Books hardcover edition January 2009

POCKET and colophon are registered trademarks of Simon & Schuster, Inc.

For information about special discounts for bulk purchases, please contact Simon & Schuster Special Sales at 1-800-456-6798 or business@simonandschuster.com

Designed by Mary Austin Speaker

Manufactured in the United States of America

10 9 8 7 6 5 4 3 2 1

Library of Congress Cataloging-in-Publication Data
Goings, Russell L.
    The children of children keep coming : a griot song / by Russell L. Goings; with illustrations by Romare Bearden. — 1st Karen Hunter Pub./Pocket Books hardcover ed.
        p.   cm.
    I. Bearden, Romare, 1911–1988.   II. Title.
    PS3607.O3455C48 2009
    811'.6—dc22   2008022078

ISBN-13: 978-1-4165-6646-5
ISBN-10:   1-4165-6646-5

To those who keep coloring our next moment

To those children who refuse to be turned from the sun of the next dawn

To the griots who sing the song

To the children of children of which I write

acknowledgments

I thank GOD for all who shared in birthing *The Children Of Children Keep Coming: An Epic Griotsong*. From early 1995 to the present, Evelyn Boulware, Dr. Kim Bridgford, Jerome Davis, and Rhodessa Goings made generous contributions to this unique song. I would also like to thank Father Thomas Regan S. J., Allan Andersen, Frank Morette, Tracy Sherrod, Karen Hunter, Brigitte Smith, Michael Ryan, and Geoff Bickford. Ancestors bow low, in lasting Homage, to them for their gifts that braid: spirituality, universality of Afro-American life with clarity and simplicity. Again thanks to all.

introduction

Sometimes there is a moment that makes you take notice.

Russell Goings's *The Children of Children Keep Coming* is the book for that moment, an epic poem that traces the journey of African-Americans in this country, that transcends pain and struggle and provides a vehicle for transformation, for weightiness that is light on its feet because of its music.

Like Walt Whitman's *Leaves of Grass*, *The Children of Children Keep Coming* reminds us of the necessity of art. People used to sit with each other and listen to poems detailing their shared cultural experience; *The Children of Children Keep Coming* is such a poem. In addition to the compelling story it tells, there is the richness of poetic devices in motion. Close your eyes. Bells are ringing; hands are clapping; feet are stomping. Over the course of the poem, motifs are picked up; a weightiness is gathered. Goings writes, "Is this the day / We pick up momentum?" If the poem itself is any indication, the answer would seem to be yes.

The Children of Children Keep Coming is a memorable book for a memorable moment.

This is not surprising, since it was written by such a remarkable man. I met Russell Goings when he visited Fairfield University in 1995, shortly after he returned from the Million Man March. A mutual friend of ours, Father Tom Regan, S. J., now the provincial of the New England Province of the Society of Jesus, suggested to Russ that he talk with me, since Russ had mentioned that he wrote poetry. I knew that he might stop by, but, as I recall, it was not a sure thing. I remember the day vividly. It was the middle of the afternoon, and I was busy grading some papers at my desk. Russ peeked around the door and introduced himself. He asked if I had a free moment. I said that I did, and welcomed him into my office. I put my pen down. We started talking. My life was never the same.

Anyone who meets Russ knows the dynamic force of his presence, which has served him well in the various successful contexts of his life—professional football player, the first African-American to hold a seat on the New York Stock Exchange, the founder of *Essence*, the friend and confidant of Romare Bearden— but what I was not prepared for was the force of the rough draft of *The Children of Children* that greeted me that day. The afternoon light shone through the window and onto his poem. There was silence as I read. Russ interrupted my reading by wondering aloud if what he had written was any good. I looked up at him. I knew I was holding a manuscript that was monumental.

We talked about many things that day—the Million Man March, poetry, his love of family, how he rose out of poverty to take on numerous challenges and surmount them. He is, after all, a man of stories. As the afternoon went on, he told me about his vision for *The Children of Children Keep Coming*, how he felt that everything that he had done in his life had led to this. I told him that he was the one to write the book, that he *had* to write the book. He paused, and then he nodded. A few days later, I was holding a new section.

This conversation went on for thirteen years, whether at Fairfield University, over the phone, or through the mail. Sometimes I would go to open my mailbox at home, and it was stuffed with pages. Many times over the years, he reminded me that, during the years of his friendship with Romare Bearden, they had a daily conversation, even as Bearden was battling cancer. When Bearden made a suggestion, Russ acted on it. That is what you do, he said, for your teacher. Such is the force of education; such is the pursuit of knowledge. You give everything to it—your time, your intelligence, your heart and soul. Daily he worked. Sometimes there would be a knock on my door at home, and I would find the mailman standing there. The manuscripts were so big they would not fit in the mailbox. Sometimes Russ read sections to me over the phone, and the music crackled over the wires. He recorded CDs—and he played all the characters—so that he could test out the interaction of the children, and see the voices join together in performance. He wrote a version of *The Children* as a play. As the years went on, Russ took many creative writing and literature classes with me—particularly the courses that had anything to do with poetry—and we held hundreds of conversations about *The Children*. *The Children* kept coming.

The voices of both real and symbolic characters speak through Goings, who is griot and prophet, a vulnerable naked soul and a writer of the epic. It is a book, it seems, he was destined to write. Every day at 3 A.M. in his apartment, he gets up to get the voices down. I often picture him there, sitting in the quietest time of New York City. I see him with his pen and paper, because he writes everything by hand. I see a man who has combated dyslexia, poverty, racism; I see a man with vision in all its various manifestations; I see a man with more than perfect vision on the football field; I see a man who used to shine shoes and who was told by the voice behind those shoes that there was something called the Stock Market; I see a man who understands money; I see a man who, as a professional football player, was fined for being late to practice because he was reading a book of poetry; I see a man who wanted to celebrate the beauty of being Black through a national magazine; I see a man who understands the heritage of Romare Bearden; I see a man who values family and friendship, who thanks God for the blessings of each day; I see a man with incredible patience, who values the importance of hard work; I see a man who believes in America. The voices speak to him, and he listens. Some are the voices of America's icons, and some are anonymous. He writes all day. Then the next day he wakes up, he listens, and he begins again.

Ultimately, Goings made a decision to use Rosa Parks as a unifying figure for the book, and rightly so. On December 1, 1955, there was a moment. Rosa Parks was tired; her feet hurt; and racism hurt. It was time. Parks took a stand by taking a seat—both on the bus and at the table of America's democracy. This is a tribute to one of America's great heroes, and Goings pays homage through the voice of the children:

You are more than kin.
We will always be true to you.
Pride and resolve lead to you.
Our fight grows with you.
We live and die with you.
There's no force that
Can separate you from us.
You are more than kin.

From her vantage point in the poem, she can look out over history and see the promise for the future:

When the Statue of Liberty turns and
Points its bright torch in our direction and
When her arms open wider
I know the great table is set.

Both visionary and quiet warrior, she is one of America's great agents for change.

In addition to the pivotal moment of Rosa Parks, Goings praises the contributions of Black women, both famous and not. They sing; they write; they encourage; they give birth. They pick everyone up; they keep going. They enrich. Harriet Tubman gets the children on the train of the Underground Railroad; Marian Anderson sings on the steps of the Lincoln Memorial; Toni Morrison writes *Sula, Song of Solomon,* and *Beloved.* Oprah Winfrey (with the beautiful pun on her name—win-free) talks, and people listen. In addition, *The Children of Children Keep Coming* has a special place in its heart for mothers. As Goings writes,

Color me woman.
Color me Black.
Color me faithful, hopeful.
Color me determined, loving.
Color my devotion eternal.
Color me mother earth.

The "I Am a Black Woman" section underscores the power of women to defy odds and to keep going for the children.

Yet men also speak of the importance of their children and of passing on their heritage. Everything is done with an eye toward the future:

God, let my son gleam in silver and gold.
Let him dream.
Let him sit under an apple tree.
Let him row from shore to shore,
Enjoying the fruits of liberty and democracy.

The poem ripples with the effects of the Million Man March, and with all the painful marches before: the march to freedom, the march to new places in history, the march to keep family together. And during that march through the generations of America's history, we hear the soulful notes of jazz and of the blues. We hear Billy Strayhorn, Duke Ellington, Louis Armstrong, and John Coltrane. We hear Dizzy Gillespie and Miles Davis. We hear Count Basie.

In addition, the book celebrates the importance of elders and history. By using the figures of Grandmother and Grandfather, Goings shows us how crucial it is that we understand and use the past. Grandmother and Grandfather frame the book, just as ancestors frame each individual. Part of this legacy is a reverence for education. Just as the elders lean on their canes, you can always lean on your education. *The Children of Children Keep Coming* is a book that celebrates knowledge:

No head is too small to birth a new thought,
No wrong is too bound to move to right.
No notion is too insignificant to stand in the head of one willing to die
For the right to hold knowledge.

It is only through a layered understanding of the past that you can be ready for the present moment and bear the promise of the future.

There are those who have been the keepers of knowledge, who have shared their knowledge, and who have created their share of moments. While many have been mentioned, there have been others: Phillis Wheatley and Sojourner Truth; Nat Turner, John Brown, and Abraham Lincoln; Ulysses S. Grant; Frederick Douglass, W. E. B. DuBois and Booker T. Washington; Prudence Crandall and her girls; Margaret Walker and Zora Neale Hurston; Malcolm X; Paul Laurence Dunbar and James Weldon Johnson; Mahalia Jackson; Rita Dove, James Baldwin, and Gwendolyn Brooks; Lead Belly and Howlin' Wolf; Marcus Garvey; Yusef Komunyakaa, Jean Toomer, and Claude McKay; Mary McLeod Bethune and Shirley Chisolm; Robert Gould Shaw and the 54th Massachusetts infantry; James Meredith; Elijah McCoy, Lewis Howard Latimer, Jan Matzeliger, and Granville T. Woods; Father Divine and Daddy Grace; Billie Holiday; Satchel Paige, Joe Louis, Jackie Robinson, and Michael Jordan; Ella Fitzgerald; James Chaney, Andrew Goodman, and Michael Schwerner; Dinah Washington and Sarah Vaughn; Adam Clayton Powell, Jr.; Madam Walker and Alice Walker; Denise McNair, Carole Robertson, Cynthia Wesley, and Addie

Mae Collins; Martin Luther King, Jr.; and the nameless people who have died and suffered and endured, who have created against all odds and added to the richness and spiritual fabric that is America. They have borne the responsibility of passing on their gifts to another generation and to the nation:

We are responsible to each other
The way the sun is to the moon,
The way the sea is to land,
The way a mother's kiss is to her child,
The way humanity is to divinity,
The way mortality is to immorality.

What we have to remember always is that it is also our cultural responsibility.

Joining these real-life figures are the symbolic characters that Goings has created to interact with history. While certainly the book can remind the reader about the lessons of history itself, it is also a poetic history, and Calli, child of the valley, Evalina, Banjo Pete, Buddy Boy, Sista Angela, Black Tiny Shiny, Mother Awareness, See See Rider, Nexus, Tellit, Ruth Brown, and Lordy, Lordy Miss Claudy join their respective voices with those you recognize. Their names are suggestive, of course, and resonate in the way that such poetic names can, and yet you recognize these other voices on another level. You come face to face with innocence, with insight, with music, with compassion. For Goings, these are real, in the way that history is real, in a rich and layered life. You also recognize the choir, Goings's chorus, which functions in the way it does in Greek drama, as commentator, participant, and social consciousness.

As the title tells us, this book is written for the children, their sense of hope and possibility and wonder. Goings's epic snaps its fingers for them; it sings for them; it offers up the lap of America; it laughs with them; it sings of equality and achievement. It offers nourishment to them, both physical and spiritual. Just listen to this passage as Goings describes earthly happiness; this is his vision for America:

See them creating under a silver moon.
On lawns hear them dancing in
The purity of new rain.
See them tasting the warmth of family love.
See them paying homage to those
Breaking barriers, opening new territories.

Or here:

Down by the riverside where flowers grow,
Where birds nest, where children play, where
Hands lock around Prometheus's light,
They hold the precious gift of life,
The gift of recording the
Songs of the soul,
The gift to appreciate the inch worm,
The soaring eagle, a copper sun,
Hot buttered beans, dancing flowers,
The gift to acknowledge
The next moment is the most precious.

It is a vision that includes everyone.

America now has such a moment. Like Walt Whitman, who is invoked throughout the poem, Goings celebrates every blade of grass and every individual. Although the poem is an epic struggle, Goings wants healing and reconciliation; togetherness and celebration. We are one America. The poem, so full of America's symbols—the flag, the Statue of Liberty, the Liberty Bell, "My Country, 'Tis of Thee"—shows their absolute necessity, and the deep feelings people have about them, even the dispossessed, perhaps especially the dispossessed. Such feelings bring tears to the eyes and hope for the future. *The Children* is not about "us" versus "them," but about togetherness, a shared cultural history, a shared present, and shared promise for the future. That's what democracy is. Goings calls America "a mosaic," with its glittering, beautiful pieces; together they make one beautiful work of art. The poem, finally, offers this message of hope:

America, heal.
We sit on the same green grass,
Sowing the colors of red, white and blue.
America, from this moment on, we drink
From the same bottomless well of Democracy.
We sit in a moment of history.
This is our country.

—Kim Bridgford
Fairfield, Connecticut
August 2008

contents

part one

Taking the Train to Freedom

Somewhere deep in the valley,
A child says:

I am born brown and black. From the ground
I come; to the ground I go back.

I'm Calli, a child of the valley,
Born in muck, bred in misery,
Carried on loved ones' backs
Through the rain and wind to the train
Where there's never a lack of love.

Holding Grandfather's arm,
Grandmother leans to him, whispering:

Do you . . . do you?
Do you hear what I hear?

The children of children are singing:

Got one mind for white folks,
Got one for me.
Got one mind for white folks,
Got one for me.
'Cause white folks don't know me.
'Cause white folks don't know me.
Got one mind for white folks,
Got one for me, that's for sure.
Got one for me.

Can you hear them calling?

My Lord, it's a beautiful sound.
Can you hear them singing?
My Lord, it's a beautiful sound.

Grandfather stands facing the sun;
He pulls his straw hat to his ears.
Dawn lights his face.
With hoe in hand, he hears the pounding
Of slaves filling the air with sounds
Of anguish.

Sometimes, on the wind, their sounds of pain
Carry from jagged mountains to meadows;
Sometimes the eerie drumbeats
Of hoes chopping cotton
Tell of slaves who fell dead.

Sometimes chained fieldhands
Bow their heads;
Sometimes they chant:

We dig no more graves.
We chop no more cotton.
We kill no more dreams.
We ruin no more seeds.

Grass grows greener
In America's democracy.

Every day,
In the sacred ground of liberty

We dig another grave.
Every day we work to end slavery.
Every day we ask God to
Stop slavery! Stop slavery now!

Every day, we the children of children
Keep coming, developing.
We keep getting stronger, wiser, smarter.
We keep advancing.
We sow more and more seeds.

Every day, we know
What it means to be Black in this country,
Where the grass grows taller,
Softer, stronger, greener for Whites.
We know Jim Crow and his crows
Affect the lives of Blacks fighting to
End slavery.

Every day,
Over open graves we,
The children of children,
Sing lullabies to the dead.

Every day,
Crows fly before us
And every day we sing:

The river is ahead;
We are not afraid,
The river is just ahead and

Every day we hear
Grandmother singing:

Just beyond the river
I hear the children of children
Moving down mountains,
Crossing poppy fields.

I hear the children of children
Gripping shovels, praising elders
Challenging crows, starting a new life.

When her spotless sack
Dress bellows in the wind,
Grandmother smiles, calling:

Come join us,
Together we'll face fate.
Together we'll open new gates.
It's never too late to spread new seeds.
We are one family.

Come, in our new home land, help us
Plow, nurture, harvest fruits.
Together we'll move beyond the river
That faces America's greening lawns.
Don't delay,
Come catch the train.

Rap-tap-rap-tap-rap
Tap-a-rap-tap-a-rap-tap
Tap-tap-tap-tap-tap.

The children of children,
Shod feet once bound
In red clay, now march.
Under ringing bells they sing:

In God's room there's
No motherless child.
The sun shines,
The Jordan rolls.
The Upper Room is never cold.

Standing under the sun of
A new day, they call:

Come, come. Come and hear
The morning rooster's song.

Come and help us break shackles,
Come and help us shape fear into resolve,
Come inside the children's circle of unity,
Come inside our circle of equality.

In fields, in deltas,
On cotton, on tobacco,
On sugarcane plantations,
The choir sings:

Where is liberty?
Where is freedom?
Where is justice and equality?

We've been down.
Today and every day
We wipe tears from our faces.
We wipe fear away.
Today and every day
Our courage abounds.

Today and every day
The children of children
Move over ground that takes them
Closer to the river where
They hear the plaintive song:

Been down too long, Lord,
Been down, just going round and round.

Lord, Lord, help us lose this frown,
Lord, we're tired of being down,
Just tired of being down.
Lord, when will we be unbound?

Lord, we see the sky, we see the sky,
Will we ever fly? Will we ever . . . fly?
Will we ever be free? Just free, Lord?
Will the train soon come by?

A mother holding her infant girl-child

To her heaving chest rocks and softly sings:

Freedom can't come soon enough.
Hold on, baby, baby.
Hold on while we seek
Higher ground. Hold on baby,
'Cause the Lord will make a way.

There is no doubt, child, no maybe,
Just hold on, child of mine.
There, there, you's my baby.
The Lord's train is always on time.

Good God Almighty
Comin' through the rain
It's the morning train that's a comin';
It's a comin'.

Baby, baby, baby.
There is no doubt, you's my only baby,
There's no maybe that's the morning train.
It's a comin', sure 'nuff,
It's a comin'.
It's a justa clickety, clickety,
Clackin', clackin', clackin'
It's justa rollin' clackin', justa clackin'.
Sweet, sweet child of mine.
Don't look behind!

Find time. Justa ride it
Ride, ride time,

Sweet, sweet child of mine.
Justa ride time; ride its rhythms,
Justa ride, ride, ride.
Time is ours to define.

In the clarity of a brilliant sun,
Evalina, mother of nine,
Tall, strong, determined,
Sings in rhyme to her children:

Our heads are no longer bowed.
Our backs are no longer bent.
Our minds are no longer spent.
Beneath the rays of the life-giving sun,
We used to walk single file.
Now, we walk and run as one.

Baby, there's no maybe,
A new day has begun.
Baby, baby
A new day brings a new sun.

Evalina guides her children
Over the terrain to the train, calling:

Lord, Lord, Lord,
The train's a comin'
Every day I hear it a comin'
It's a comin' through a tunnel.

With bundles on her back,

She stumbles into a clear running river.
Those already wading, wail:

Sista, wade deeper,
Wade further, wade wider.

Today and every day we wash
Ourselves in the river,
Where we offer a lullaby, by and by,
Where the rooster sings,
Where blackbirds fly,
Where babies cry.

Evalina tells her children:

Abide,
We are advancing, soon we'll be
Down by the riverside where
Fettered feet refuse to retreat.

Come,
We leave no one behind.
All will catch Freedom's Train.

Mothers join Evalina,
Standing in the sunshine.
While Banjo Pete, her husband, strums,
Evalina, holding buckets, instructs:

Pick up your buckets,
Fill them with sunshine,

It's time to get on board.

Hear the conductor callin',
Come one and all, we are going
Beyond the river;
You, you, and you get on board.

In another part of the cotton field,
Banjo Pete's music reverberates:

Now that the bossman's bags are full,
We better fill our bags before we steal away.
We better fill them before the train comes.
We better fill them, stacking them side by side.
We better fill our bags with food and supplies.

Maudell Sleet, with strong shoulders,
Sure hands, and quick feet,
Joins her grandson, Banjo Pete,
They recite:

We fill bags while fording
Deeper and wider streams,
While keeping dreams alive.
We fill them, all of them, with dreams
Of sweet milk and cream.

Stay alive, just stay alive. Just survive.
Truth is alive, truth cannot die.
Survive, justa survive.

Banjo Pete turns to his grandmother,
Maudell Sleet, and sings:

We better fill the bossman's bags
With cotton balls of shame,
Before the seasons change.
We better fill them 'cause
When he learns we's on the train,
From this day on
Things will never be the same.

In the distance,
Over the sound of the train,
A chorus of workers slavin' instructs:

Help those who are lame,
Help those who hold a claim,
Help those with shackled feet.
Help those who refuse defeat.

We fill quotas in the morning dew,
We fill them before curfew,
We fill bags from morning to dusk.
Now is the time to
Fill our bags, fill them full.

Build strength.
Swim, run, climb, walk, wait, plan.
Grow stronger,
Get closer to the river.
Be careful when dodging bullets,

Bang-bang-bang-bang-bang.

Through spring and summer,
Through fall and winter,
We wait for the spring's thaw.
Soon we'll cross the river
To lush level lawns.

Year after year
There have been trains,
Slow trains, fast trains,
Long trains, short trains,
To take us to the river
Facing the lawns of democracy.

Year after year
There have been trains,
Mule trains, pony trains,
Horse trains,
Blue trains, gray trains,
Trains coming through rain and sleet,
Trains coming side by side.

Still, we wait, still we wait
Down by the riverside.

Just beyond the river,
Trains come weaving hope.
They come knowing
They won't be slowed down for long.
They come singing the song of life.

Under sun high and moon low,
The children of children rise to sing:

Mother, father, sister, brother,
Aunt, uncle, lover:
Is this the day?
Is this the day we start a new life?
Is this the day we stand on dry ground?
Is this the day we catch the train?
Is this the day we rearrange the score?
Is this the day we open the door?
Is this the day freedom's bell
Rings to include
Black, brown, tan, light, white?

Hallelujah, hallelujah,
Lord, Lord, Lord,
Is this the day?
Is this the day we no longer hide?
Is this the day we come to
Help hasten the slow train?
Is this the day we are told
Why we must go beyond the river?

Clapping and stomping their feet,
They shout:

Heavenly Father,
Is this the day when gangs in chains
No longer hammer?

Is this the day when brothers and sisters
No longer dodge Jim Crow and his crows?
Is this the day winter starts to thaw?
Is this the beginning of spring?

Heavenly Father,
Is this the day when mothers and fathers
Stop digging graves,
Stop burying sons and daughters.
Is this the day to start:
Weeding, growing, owning, building?

Lord, dear Lord,
Is this the day when wheels turn?
Is this the day we drink clear water?
Is this the day the green grass of democracy
Begins to grow under our feet?

Under sun high and moon low,
The question is asked:

Is this the day drums:
Rap-rap-rap-rap-rap
Tap-a-rap-tap-rap-tap
Rap-rap-rap-rap-rap?

Is this the day
To stop hiding under cellar doors,
To stop hiding in thickets and cane fields?
Is this the day the caged bird
Stops bruising his fluttering wings

Against the bars of injustice?
Is this the day the caged bird
Stops singing off-key?

Is this the day in the morning tide,
In the noon tide, in the evening tide,
During low and high tide we follow
Harriet Tubman?

Is this the day
We pick up momentum,
We move over the marshes,
We move down the mountainside?
Is this the day
To follow a new stream?

Is this the day we follow Harriet Tubman?

The woman called Moses is
Listening to a young boy runnin', runnin'.
She hears on the
Winds of his parents' angst:

Lord, it's our son, Buddy Boy,
A rope tied around his waist,
Hope in his eyes,
He's puffin,' runnin',
Avoidin' the patrollers.

His parents call:

The lynch rope is justa
Hangin', hangin' from saddles.

Through a thorny bush,
The boy sees Harriet.
He hears the patrollers' horses gallop by:

Klippity, klop,
Klippity, klop.
Klop. Klop.

He cries:

They's comin'.
They's justa klippity, klippity,
They's justa klop, klop, kloppin'.

Mama, Mama,
I see the rope a danglin'
I hear the rope a tappin'.

It's singin', readyin'
Waitin', swingin' swayin,'
Justa wantin' me.

With fear on his face, he calls:

Mama, Mama
Tell my sisters and brothers,
Every day, look up in the sky,

See me rounding Cape of Horn,
Know I crossed the Atlantic.

Tell them to hear my song,
I stand knowin' I'm right,
Slavin' is wrong.

Mama, tell all
To stand in the daylight.
Soon we'll meet down by the riverside
Where the spirit of Emmett Till resides,
Where the Scottsboro Boys'
Innocence rides high covering the
Entire blue sky.

Buddy Boy's sister, Angela,
A willowy gifted dancer, pleads:

Mother,
Can we go to him?
Can we help him escape?

Angela smoothes her crinkled sack dress.
She pulls threads; she unties knots;
She beats back fear and asks:

Has Buddy Boy
Gone to lie down?
Is he still in the hay?
Is he on the train?

Is he with Harriet?
Is he underground?
Is he on the railroad?
Is he at the river?
Is the river at high tide?

Just before the river
I see bees fluttering, crows cawing;
I hear wheels.

Mama, Mama,
Is that the sound of The Freedom's Train
I hear comin' around terrain?

Buddy Boy, no gust of wind in your face
Can beat you back.
Brother, you'll survive,
You'll get to the river.

Mama, I hear you say our brother
Nexus is on his way.

Nexus shouts:

Buddy Boy's long arms embrace
More than a dream; he's crossin'
Deepening ponds, lakes, and streams.

Nexus pulls a dirt-spotted blue shirt
To his lean body.
His tattered white pants,

Splattered with red mud, flap
In rhythm with his anxiety.
Nexus hears:

Pat-rap-pat-pat
Pitty-pat-pitty-pat-pat-pitty.
Rap-rap-rap-pat-rap
Pat-pat-pat-pat-rap.
Tap, tap, tap.

Mothers and fathers chant:

We hear your advice:
Leave, migrate,
Answer the call, stand tall.
We hear you calling:
Leave with everything
You have on your backs,
Catch the train.

Angela speaks, saying:

Listen to my brothers.
They are telling us,
It's never too late to march another mile,
It's never too late to rock the cradle,
It's never too late to gather the reins.

It's never too late to kneel when prayin',
It's never too late to love a motherless child.
It's never too late to enter God's room.

It's never too late to be baptized in the Jordan.
It's never too late to praise God on bent knees.

A young mother, wading in a gentle stream,
Holding her new baby, sighs:

Do you hear the brothers?
Child, child of mine,
We's gonna be fine.
Hallelujah, hallelujah, hallelujah,
The brothers are laying new tracks!

They's calling:
Come, come, come this way.
Come, take our hands.
Come, leave darkness and fear,
The river is near.

Come, leave slavery now.
Come cross a starless sky.
Come support our creation.
Come help us form a better nation.

Under sun high and moon low,
The children of children fuse and weld their will
To never run again from the gun.

They weave multicolored quilts,
Quilts fashioned from threads
Of those who made the last run,
For those who will make the next run,

Quilts now worn by those confronting
Jim Crow and his crows.

Conductors on Freedom's trains call:

We protect, we direct.
We detect, we correct.
We align what needs aligning.
We provide books with instructions.
We build bridges; we smooth ridges.

We are experts in tiptoeing
On bare feet,
Over hot sand,
Over jagged precipices.

From a barn, a mother, holding eggs, calls:

I hear the children of children.
Their drums: rap-rap-rap-rap-rap.
Their feet: tap-tap-tap-tap-tap.
Their hands: clap-clap-clap-clap-clap.

I see them linking more than hands.
They are chanting, answer the call.
Cross the Mason-Dixon Line.
Someday soon we'll move
From the back to the front.

Someday soon
We'll shout and turn about saying:

Freedom, freedom is fine,

Freedom never confines, nor is it ever blind.

Someday soon we won't always be the last in line.

From fields, workers

Hoein', choppin', carryin', holler:

Hear the bossman sayin':

Not today, nigga!

Someday you'll get your full pay.

Not today nigga!

Remember the Ku Klux Klan

Will never go away; we's here to stay.

We's here to . . .

Field hands call:

We stand hand to hand,

Shoulder to shoulder.

We raise our worn straw hats,

We wipe sweat from brows,

We will not go away without our full pay.

The bossman says:

You niggas have credit with me.

Believe me, there ain't no need to count.

I keep the books,

For sure I know the score, you'll

Always owe me.
Your account is secure.
Just keep buying from my store.

The choir of field workers calls:

Bossman, answer this:
Why is our count always short,
Our obligations to you long?
Why are our days endless with sweat,
Our nights full with threats?
Why can't we ever get out of debt?

Why is our pay always late?
Why do you always determine our fate?
Why are your credits always taken on time?
Why is gettin' our accurate pay
Always an act of faith?
Why is payday's pay
Always a day away?

Linked as one, workers call:

We come over mountains,
We come through fields of red,
We come through fields holding our dead.
We come in homage
Over the graves of the once enslaved,
Spooling stronger thread.

We are responsible to each other
The way the sun is to the moon,
The way the sea is to land,
The way a mother's kiss is to her child,
The way humanity is to divinity,
The way mortality is to immortality.

We are responsible to each other
The way spring is to summer,
The way trust is to honor,
The way honesty is to fidelity,
The way spirituality is to eternity,
The way eternal is to everlasting.

We are responsible to each other
The way the sun nourishes,
The way a mother shares,
The way fingertips knit togetherness,
The way absence of freedom braids longing.

We are responsible to each other
The way time spins,
The way a nipple is to suckle,
The way a lip is to kiss,
The way lovers' hearts skip,
The way emotions dip and flip.
The way race is to diversity,
The way integration is to controversy.

Under sun high and moon low
Freedom's train is justa comin'.

Clickety-clack-clack-clickety-clack, clacking.
It's carryin' Moses
And Moses is justa conductin' and callin':

Freedom. Freedom.
All aboard. All aboard.
I'm here. Hear me, come,
There's room here.

My riders come from farms and fields,
From towns and hamlets;
Their feet a movin', justa tappin',
Mothers just a rockin', nursin' and babies cryin',
Sisters, brothers, aunts, and uncles
Justa comin', justa tryin',
Justa preparin', justa travelin', justa leavin'.

Over the anger of slavers screaming:

Nigger we'll kill you if you try to escape,
Workers sing:
Freedom! Freedom!
Moses is conducting.
Freedom's train is coming for us.
All come aboard.

Moses's train travels above ground,
Underground, on high dry ground,
On firm ground.

With Harriet conducting
Its doors are always open,

Its wheels are always creating distance
Between freedom and slavery.

Under sun high and moon low
A wise grandmother, a storyteller
Sings of leaving slavery:

It's the sweet old story that unfolds as it's told.
It's the sweet old story that never grows old.
It's the story told when nights are long.
It's the sweet old story told in drumbeats,
In footsteps leaving slavin',
Tap-tap-trap-trapping.

It's the sweet old story that's told in a
Familiar embrace, that has no race.
It's the story told by hands, hands
That color belief, hands that provide relief.

Grandmother fingers a rock
When she rocks in her favorite chair.
In the calm of twilight, she whispers:

It's the sweet old story that
Sets tables, that arranges chairs.
It's the story of buttered beans,
Cornpone, collard greens, hot
Sweet potato pie.

It's the story of prayer.
It's the sweet old story of

Moses and Sojourner Truth
Safely guiding
Freedom's train to the promised land.

It's the sweet old story of
The children of children, Harriet,
Truth, Turner, Brown, Lincoln,
Grant, Shaw, the 54th.

It's the sweet old story of
Grandmother and Grandfather,
Evalina and Buddy Boy,
Banjo Pete and Maudell Sleet,
Douglass, Tellit, Garvey, Booker T.,
DuBois, Powell, King, Wells.

It's the story of bravery, of strugglers
Planting seeds, of growing green grass.
It's the story of democracy, liberty, unity.
It's the story that ends slavery,
That begins freedom, justice, equality.

It's the story of humanity.
It's the story of making the journey beyond the river.
It's the story of turning
Wrong to right, darkness to light.

God's ministers sweeping the heavens,
Preach to the children of children:

Retrieve your drums thrown down wells.

Make music where there's none.

Oppose tyranny.

Oppose Jim Crow and his crows.

Oppose bigoted mores, racial and religious bias.

Calli rises, her voice singing:

On bent knees,

We master a new language.

We redirect shame, hurt and pain.

On lips, in gestures, in dance.

We master the story

Of exodus and revolution, our

Victory over oppression.

We pick up sticks and stones,

We build bridges, tracks and homes.

We unearth new phrases,

We stand the weak with the strong.

Calli intones:

With Ethos and Pathos

Deepening the color of our blood we

Arrange, harmonize, meld

Scales, bars, half-notes, whole notes.

We channel impatience into creativity,

Where the beginning of an aesthetic is modest.

We blend the silence that

Death brings to the next moment with
Toms, drums, sticks, racks,
High-hats, rhythm, meter.

Rap-rap-tap-tap-tap, begins
With the heart and mind joining to
Express the music of our soul.

On Freedom's train, riders
See a father pressing
A baby to his blood-stained
Shirt, shouting:

Hallelujah, hallelujah,
My child is God's child.

Trumpets play down by the riverside,
Where all celebrate the song
That frees the spirit
From the death of slavery.

In our new land of liberty, we shout:

Nobody knows the trouble we see,
Nobody knows but you and me.
Nobody knows the trouble we see.
Crows surround you and me,
Killing Blacks, by ones, by twos, by threes.

In dim lights, under safe roofs,
Mothers and fathers tell the story:

How Harriet's bell calls day and night,
How she keeps out of sight,
How riders on her train
Come by ones, by twos, by threes.

When they take flight she calls,
Hold tight, no soul is ever left behind.
Every day Harriet's riders
In rain, in sleet, in snow, in sunshine
Cross Jim Crow's bloody land, leaving
Slavery behind.

Maudell Sleet, Billy Boy and Banjo Pete
Follow the North Star shining on
Freedom seekers on Moses's train.

They see Harriet's long dress
Sweeping the ground.
They hear her soft voice filling shanties.
They grow still when she fingers
The trigger of her rifle.
They sigh, deep with relief, when she calls:

All aboard, break from slavery.
Come from under the weeping willow tree,
No one ever died while traveling with me.

Her riders feel the moment;
Their hearts throb,
Their feet tremble,

Their emotions erupt,
Their bodies bend in the wind.
Enslavement crumbles.

Harriet's train enters
The land of tall healthy greening grass.
The steady beat of rejoicing voices sing:

Rap-rap-tap-tap-rap.

In the sky red, white and blue bandanas
Shimmy over green lawns.
Freedom riders call:

All aboard. All aboard.
Freedom is ahead.
Only slavery's tracks in back,
Nothing can turn us back.

Cawing crows cover the sky;
Moses points the rifle:

Crack!

The hammer of the rifle sings
The music of Harriet's resolve.
The duet of the
Hammer's crack and her voice
Is heard in shanties,
In fields, in minds and hearts:

My call is to the young and old.
Getting on board is up to you and me.

She whispers:

Move to freedom.
Hurry! Be quiet.
There is no charge.
Move to freedom.

At first light, rise with the sun in your face.
Follow the expanding edge of green grass.
Step on the lawns of democracy.
You are free.
You are free.

Under sun high and moon low,
The children of children getting off the train
Hear Sista Angela praying:

Lord, Lord, Lord.
Been down, down, down.
Lord, been down so long.
Now, with you at my side,
I rise, I rise, I rise.
Every day I rise.
I rise on the pulse of the morning.
I rise out of darkness to sing.

I rise to know the first blush of spring.
I rise to fill spring with fresh song,

With rhythm, with dance, with a steady beat.
I rise knowing, like seasons, colors change.
I rise, coloring new experiences with
Freedom, liberty, democracy.

I rise making my way to the North Star,
To the Promised Land.
Today and every day
I rise knowing it's the first day of life's journey.
I rise knowing my star is gonna shine, shine, shine.

I rise to birth, to be reborn.
I rise to live out fate.
I rise exercising faith.

On this day I rise to proclaim,
No more auction block for us,
No more slavin',
No more chain gang,
No more bullwhip,
No more open graves.
Below hanging tree.

This day, we The Children of Children
Change forever I to We.

We rise! We rise! We rise!
We rise to stand with Sojourner Truth,
We rise to stand with Harriet Tubman.
We rise to reset the clock.
We rise to meet the power of a new beginning.

At sunrise the grieving country sees
Wilting lilacs surrounding him,
The earth claiming dust.
President Lincoln is dead.
Voices call:

Lincoln's death will delay the day's sunrise.
Oh Lord, what a morning.
Oh Lord, what a mourning.

Is it his time to die?
Is it his time? It's our time.
We must rise, rise, rise as one!

The chill of the mourning dew saturates
Browning, floating lilacs.
Bound to grief; the country dawdles,
Crows hide in coops,
The Stars and Stripes droop.

The children of children keep coming;
They keep getting stronger.
The nation sings:

Under our flag of unity, it's time
To level the nation's lawns.
We rise to open ears, minds and hearts.
We rise to cherish a united country.
We rise to color democracy's grass inclusive.

The children of children chant
The nation's blues song:

He's gone, gone, gone.
Death took something we own.
Our president has gone home;
Just gone . . .

The country hums
Words that find their way into seams,
Words that ride down slopes,
Words that fill time,
Words that heal:

One nation,
One flag,
One people seeding the fallow.

Just beyond the river,
Blueswomen and Bluesmen sing:

Weep no more, weep no more.
Lay your burden down.
Sweep away tears, lilacs are abloom.

Down by the riverside,
New songs rise to thrive
In honky-tonks,
In dives, at fish fries.
Down by the riverside,
Mournful voices rise singing the Blues:

Mama! Mama, please, sing that song to me.
I hold fast the thinning threads
That hold me and you to the past.

Mama, please sing that song to me.
I long to sit again under the mango tree.
Long ago I was the first to leave.
You know Buddy Boy is never slow.

Mama,
From under a cottonwood tree,
The bluesman Howlin' Wolf sings:
Baby, don't leave,
Come back to my shack.
The Klan's on the attack.

Mama,
I hear you singing:
Baby, I know you miss your
Pig's feet, fried corn, fried fish,
Apple pie and honey.

Listen to the new lady directing the train.
Ma Rainey's saying more than grace.
She hums:

Take me where the sun is always bright,
A place where freedom is always in bloom,
A place where commitments are always honored,
Take me where liberty is a constant parade.
Take me where fidelity is nurtured in a womb,

Where it can't be entombed,

Where it's never just beyond the river.

Where Freedom is never in the shade.

Take me where

Loyalty is more than a ripple.

Take me where

No whisper is too soft to hear,

No distance too far to travel,

No river, lake, pond, or stream is

Too wide, too deep, too shallow to cross.

Under sun high and moon low,

Lying flat on our naked backs,

We hear feet, bare feet crossing deserts.

We recognize crows waiting in rivers, ponds, streams.

We hear chains of slavery breaking,

We hear voices calling:

Escape we must, in God we trust.

Lord, why is there no guide we can trust?

Under sun high and moon low,

Stranded in a new nation, we sing:

We've known rivers once forgotten,

Ancient dusty rivers,

Rivers where huts meet the tide,

Where the enslaved won't be denied.

Lord,

Why is there no sun?

Why are we always facing the gun?
Why are crows sitting on our morrow?
Why no sparrows, only sorrow?

Throughout the country,
Parading Black soldiers shout:

In this land of democracy
Why is unrestricted freedom so
Slow coming to us? Why must we wait?
One, two, three,
Some gotta die,
Some of us will die to be free.
One, two, three.
We fight, we die.
Our feats leave lasting prints
In history's memory.

Parading soldiers sing:

Gotta walk back some and build support,
Gotta turn away from disgrace,
Gotta give tolerance and understanding space.
Gotta exhibit grace.

Gotta feel rap-rap-rap-rap-pat,
Gotta feel the rhythms of life,
Gotta hear the drums sing.

Gotta drink sweet water from deep new wells.
Gotta create new music.

Gotta master different scores.

Gotta write black and white notes.

Gotta stomp our feet, clap our hands, sing our song.

Gotta hold tight, tighter; even when dying.

The children of children call:

Gotta feel the holy spirit

Before we can speak in our tongue.

Gotta walk faster,

Gotta master knowledge,

Gotta harness our collective intelligence.

Gotta muster all our forces.

Gotta feel the rain that soaks the earth

With our blood.

Gotta make music out of songs the cicadas sing,

Gotta cup the ears of the newborn,

Gotta keep our ears appreciating

The original, the unique.

Gotta tie and untie

What is and what is not possible.

Gotta hear the songs the guardian

Of liberty sings:

Gotta keep creating.

Gotta keep workers' hands digging deeper.

Gotta keep our eyes recognizing value.

Black souls praying for the soldiers chant:

Gotta know:
There ain't no helpless too lame to defend,
There ain't no lip too tight to pray,
There ain't no day too short or too long
To find the way to democracy,
Liberty, equality, justice.

It is the responsibility of
The children of children to teach:

No one is never too
Short, too fat, too thin, too tall
To drink from the deepening well of democracy.
No leg is too short, too long, too weak
To carry the message
Of freedom, justice, equality.
No lawn is ever too bumpy to make level.
We vow to make America's
Rough dirt spots green with grass.

No lip is too thin to speak the truth.
No lie can keep truth from raising the roof.
No lie can withstand undeniable proof.
No lie will shine with eternal light.

Ruth Brown, a singing storyteller declares:

Never will one have more freedom than another.
Never will we abandon honor, respect, duty.
Never will we forget the meaning of
Brother, sister, mother, father.

Never will we forget we are
Keepers of tradition, heritage,
Keepers of culture,
Keepers of the torch of freedom,
Keepers who burnish
Freedom's light making it
Clearer, larger, brighter, fairer.

Parading Black soldiers call:

Sacred is the ground at Fort Wagner,
At Fort Pillow, at Harper's Ferry.
From the dust we come,
To the dust we go back.
The ground holds our dead.
Sacred are our pledges to them:

Never will there be a day
When it's too long, too busy,
Too short for us to pray.

Never will a day come
When it's too hot, too cold to give praise.

Never will our feet be too blistered,
Too sore to carry one more
Soul to freedom's shore.

Never will we be too satisfied
To meet a new sunrise.

Never will we be too secure
To help one more.

The commander of the 54th Massachusetts infantry,
Robert Gould Shaw,
Dressed in the colors of Old Glory, calls:

We know green grass.
We are ready to die defending it.
We will die, fighting to protect
Democracy's grass.

Commitment, duty, honor
Is for all citizens.
Democracy must never fall.
Soon, freedom for all!

All must parade in step, in this civil war,
By ones, twos, threes.
Dawn brings blazing guns,
Black and White men
Running to face the revealing sun.

Soon death's shadows flicker,
Soon our spirit takes flight,
Soon death,
Soon the earth registers its claim.

Over Fort Wagner, Black voices call:

Our nation can't divide itself.
We are black, white, brown, yellow,
Just men and women, protecting,
Marching, ending slavery.

On this day, July 18, 1863,
Parading Black men dressed in
The blue uniform of the Union shout:

Hear us, we are one in duty.
Duty always exacts a price.
Duty is carrying those who can't
Defend freedom, liberty, justice,
On democracy's green lawns.
Duty is to remain one people
In an undivided nation.
It's our duty to run over sacred ground.
It's our duty to carry the nation's colors.
It's our duty to stand tall and advance.
It's our duty to face the many faces of
Evil peering from Fort Wagner's walls.

Death doesn't discriminate.
The earth holds ashes.
Death doesn't discriminate.
America sighs, citizens cry:

Oh! Lord, trouble is on its way,
Please come by here.
Trouble is on the way,
Lord, please come by here.

The children of children speak:

Lord, it's cold;
Make the rain stop.
Let the sun's rays warm us.
Keep the colors in the nation's flag bright.

A mother and father call:

Hold on son.

They hear their son,
In a high black top hat, preaching:

I'm keeping the faith.
I'm holding on, holding on.
I'm keeping the faith.
There's no doubt, no maybe,
I'll always keep the faith baby.

The face of duty, commitment,
Honor I live by.
They reign day and night.
The ground is wet with the blood
Of those fighting, dying, while
Exercising
Faith, duty, commitment, honor.

Facing death they pray:

Lord, we are one with you and your son
One people, one with President Lincoln.
Bless all answering the call.
Fate has cast the moment.

Parents on bent knees join the preacher in prayer:

Our fighting loved ones carry the lamp of freedom.
It's the lamp that starts the day.
It's the lamp of the nation's courage.
It serves families, it serves our country.
It will glow until slavery is no more, no more.
Its intense glow shows the way.

Hands of families and friends
Held high in supplication,
Point to those saying:

The lamp of victory is swinging,
The red, white and blue is flying.
Light is shining on blue birds,
On black birds, on white birds.
Bees are pollinating, flowers are swaying.
Citizens are coming together to sing:
We are one in spirit, one in soul,
One in America's belief in freedom.
The claim to freedom's light
Is the same for all.

Frederick Douglass stands before the country preaching:

One strand of green grass is equal to another;
Our nation is not in disarray.
No adversity can tear us apart.
We are a country proud of diversity.
This day is our day, July 18, 1863.

From all over the country, voices call:

Under our nation's flag,
We pledge we won't let the 54th die.
Soon freedom's flag will fly.

We know freedom can't wait.
The weight of the truth
Tips the scale from wrong to right.

Teachers in schools sing:

Three cheers for the 54th of Massachusetts.
Three cheers for the four who earned
The Gilmore medal for valor during the
Assault on Fort Wagner.

Sacred are the steps of the brave men of the 54th,
Men who died closing the distance between
Slavery and freedom.
Death extracts, subtracting
One more from the living.

Their lifeless bodies
Shine in Savannah, in Memphis, in Atlanta,
In hamlets, in towns, in cities, in villages
Under the weeping willow trees.

General Ulysses S. Grant decries:

God rues the man called Forrest, Nathan Forrest,
The devil leader of the men and women in gray.
At Fort Pillow General Forrest orders:
Shoot, burn alive,
Kill all, kill children, women,
Kill the infirm, the crippled.
Let the ground grow soggy with nigga blood.
There's no surrender.

The children of children sing:

Sacred is the ground
On which we fall.
In death we answer the call.
Death and life is the same for all.
Sacred is the light that shines on Fort Pillow.

We come in spirit, in prayer, bringing light.
We come believing in God's might.
Right's light is never high for you and low for me.
Right's flames ford
Streams and rivers, seas and oceans,
Minds and hearts, intentions and perceptions.

President Lincoln once said: Tell the nation,
Colonel Shaw and the men of the 54th,
Storming Fort Wagner's gate,
Did not die in vain.
Today the North and South gate of hate falls.
Slavery ends.

Under sun high and moon low,
A lone soldier intones:

Today, June 18, 1863,
Muffled drums roll.
Life goes cold.
Bullets remold.
Struck bodies fold.
Deeds scroll.
Blood forms shoals.
Death takes its toll.

From within the gate of Fort Wagner,
Colonel Shaw calls:

Come, be you Black or White.
Together we'll raise the red, white and blue
In Vicksburg, Mississippi,
In New Orleans, Louisiana, in Atlanta, Georgia,
In misshapen hearts,
In minds, in the attitude of Dixie Land.
Unfurl the Stars and Stripes.
Over the evil of slavery.

Through blood-soaked cracks,
The seeds planted at Harper's Ferry,
Fort Wagner, Fort Pillow begin to sprout
Before the giant to come, Rosa Parks.

I will not move
I will stay in this seat.

Voices of ancestors shout:
Don't move!

On the bus, filled with crows,
The lady called Parks
Tells the children of children:

Every day I hear the men of the 54th
Coloring hope passionate,
Coloring determination endless,
Forging, fighting, advancing.
I see the men reclaiming dignity,
Firming human rights.

I hear Colonel Shaw saying:
Spring will bring a thaw;
Slavery will be no more.

Clapping her hands,
Rosa Parks proclaims:

Colonel Shaw is an old friend.
My spirit is that of the men of the 54th

There is never a day
When I don't feel their spirit.

When crows surround the segregated bus,
Rosa Parks hears the echo of the 54th:

Don't move, you are blessed with grace,
Keep the sun in your face,
Don't turn away.
Your journey began June 18, 1863.

History's pace can never rest.
Our spirit guides and protects you.
Let no shadow fall on your quest
Still we sit with you
Facing the same hatred that peered
From the oppressors of Black freedom.

The faces of those waiting with Rosa Parks
Are the same faces of Black pride
That faced Fort Wagner and Fort Pillow.

The children of children call to her:

Your light will never go out,
You shine day and night.

Rosa Parks sings:

Our fate is in our hands.
We face guns, denial,
Discrimination, death.

This morning,
There is no mourning,
There's no debate.
I will not move from this seat.

The children of children sing:

You are more than kin.
We will always be true to you.
Pride and resolve lead to you.
Our fight grows with you.
We live and die with you.
There's no force that
Can separate you from us.
You are more than kin.

A knowing smile enters her face;
She sighs, sets deeply, and hums:

Time quickly passes,
Today's sun is not the last I'll see.
Pale grass, in time, will soon turn bright green,
How quickly morning turns to noon.

Around the bus the sun shines on bright green lawns.
She speaks:

I know this is the first of many bus rides.

Sprouts of green sway,
The red, white and blue waves,

Crows caw,
Kneeling children sing:

Oh, say can you see
In a new century, Rosa Parks
Refusing to move?
She is securing a seat for you and me.

Under sun high and moon low,
In one voice they shout:

We know,
No head is too small to birth a new thought,
No wrong is too bound to move to right.
No notion is too insignificant to stand in the head
Of one willing to die for the
Right to hold knowledge.

We feel the power of insight,
We know freedom is not physical;
We must hold it tight.

The children of children
Carrying books, carrying the word
Hear Sista Awareness calling:

Learn, baby, learn.
Learn all you can.
Step the step.
Step the strut of those who learn.

Baby, when you step,
You can never get enough to learn.

Look at the three sisters,
Awareness, Understanding, Insight
Strutting in front of the Apollo, singing out:

Learning comes on foot, by train and boat.
It comes scarred and tattered, on worn shoes.
Its gospel is preached in schools and pools.

The children of children join
Others toiling, fighting, learning.
They chant:

We come open and eager to learn,
We come refusing nothing
That will help us defeat
Jim Crow and his crows.

We come knowing
Streams flow,
Deeds weave,
Learning bridges,
Knowledge is power,
Respect is earned,
Dignity is worn,
Freedom is won.

We come knowing,
Within us the fire burns,

Praying delivers,
Goodness endures,
Evil can never win.

Every day, while waiting, the children of children
Shape bits and pieces of knowledge into belief.
They chant:

We learn, we work, we experience,
We exercise insight, understanding,
Wisdom, and intelligence.
We work to overcome the impossible.

Every day Lincoln, Douglass,
Truth, Tubman, Buddy Boy,
Evalina, Banjo Pete,
Maudell Sleet, Black Tiny Shiny call:

Freedom always looks ahead.
Freedom floats, glides, and
Flows from here to there.
Freedom grows from a
Ripple to a wave, to laws ending slavery.

Freedom, freedom,
Freedom supports
A delegation,
A congregation,
A nation.
Freedom builds a home for you and me.
Humanity must be free.

Freedom has
Legs, arms, a body, a mind,
A soul, a spirit.

Freedom can never rest when it's at its best.

In this land, our land, we share
Freedom's gospel knowing,
Sometimes freedom comes crawling, limping,
Sometimes freedom comes walking, running,
Sometimes freedom comes mending, gathering.

Sometimes freedom comes scarred and tattered,
Sometimes freedom comes down by the
Riverside, where hands are washed,
Where hands row, hoe, chop, pull, tow,
Where black struggling hands clap and snap,
Keeping freedom's meter perfect.

On the lawns of democracy,
In a rousing voice,
The nation sings:

Notes, notes, notes, harmonizing notes.

We ain't gonna
Carry no more broken
Promissory notes
We gonna cash notes,
Half notes, quarter notes, eighth notes,
Full notes, black and white notes.

We gonna rearrange notes,
Acknowledging their full value
To remove pain and shame.

We ain't gonna sing broken notes no more.
We ain't gonna play broken notes no more.
We ain't gonna hold broken notes no more.

No more will we live in fear.
We come wearing hope, we come
Spreading faith, we come preaching the gospel,
Seeding what's right.
We come firing our spirits.

In America we share green grass,
Tulips, bees, butterflies.
In America, never again
Slavery in America.

America's light is gonna
Shine, shine, shine.

Under sun high and moon low,
The light is passed.
Buddy Boy gives it to Black Tiny Shiny.
Black Tiny Shiny gives it to Sojourner Truth.
They rejoice:

Shine, shine, shine.
Let the light shine.
On all my people,
Black, fertile, beautiful.

With the sun in their faces,
They recite:

Like black topsoil we birth generations
Rich in originality,
Rich in creativity,
Rich in spirituality.

Every day on the lawns of democracy,
We work to deepen roots of freedom,
To stand taller with dignity,
To move closer to equality,
To balance justice fairer and firmer.

Black Tiny Shiny exclaims:

Nothing more! Nothing more!
We come believing in this country
That proclaims
Liberty, justice, equality, democracy,
Freedom for all its citizens.
We come demanding full access to the
Ripe fruits of freedom.

Hear my prayer:

Nothing less! nothing less!
Lord, on bent knees,
We thank you for helping us to
Keep strange fruit from
Swinging in the breeze.

Every day Jim Crow and his crows yell:

Blacks, we are ready . . . for you.
More and more
Decaying fruit will hang in leafless trees.
Hanging black ornaments entertain us.
America is the land of the the Ku Klux Klan!

Run, nigga, run.
We burn niggas like you.
In our country there's no liberty,
No peace for niggas.

Blacks answer:

We will not flee.
The murdering must stop.
We are free.

Every day we lessen the pitter-patter
Of oppression and
Every day we cleanse the grime of injustice
From the nation's windows.

Our resolve welds:
Rap-rap-rap-rap-pat
Pat-tat-pat-tap-pat-tat-tat
Pat-pat-pat-pat-tat.

We come learning, developing, believing,
Singing and mixing, drumming and humming.

We come performing in a band, we come
Fighting the Klan, fighting the Klan.

Throughout America,
Let our people go is heard
In the footsteps of those
Carrying bags across the
Bad land of the Klan.

Black Tiny Shiny
Leads the children of children in song:

Shame and sorrow burns intensely within us.
Where is the glory of liberty?
Where is America's democracy?

Every day down by the riverside
We bathe in the healing mist
That begins to dull the stain of slavery.

Gabriel's praying washes us
In the blood of the lamb.
Singing through his horn, he calls:

Precious Lord take our hand.
While we wait on the rock of ages
Lord, we beseech you to
Cut down trees that bear strange fruit.
Lord, why no rest for the weary?

When rebuked and scorned we linked hands,

Determined to advance to the center of
Flourishing green lawns.

For years we created music that soothed the soul,
Music that strengthened our resolve for equality
In America's expanding democracy.

Dressed in black,
Hair tied in a bun at the back,
Mahalia Jackson sings:

God's gospel is the song I sing;
I don't sing the Blues.

We stand together under one flag.
It's up to you and me to clear the air
Segregation is not God's notion of fair.

From across the land, I hear voices calling:
Lord, Lord, let Black people go.
Lord, Lord, let there be no more
Capturing, hanging, swinging, burning,
No more twisting bodies.

Under sun high and moon low,
The children of children shout:

Did you listen to the president
When he called:

Over new paths
Black and White hands are
Pointing the way to a new day.

When Mahalia hears the president, she
Claps and shouts:

Hallelujah, hallelujah.
Walk, children.
Don't get weary, 'cause one day
We gonna lay our burdens down.
We gonna wear our crown and gown.
Children, no one can turn us around.

We gonna roll on, roll on,
Black and White working together,
Learning new facts, laying new tracks.
Clickety clack, clack, clickety clack, clack.
Roll together, children, don't ever move back.

Our nation is best
Exploring purple mountains and
Laboring in amber waves of grain,
That hold fast beneath the feet of
All its citizens.

Rejoicing, the nation sings:

Freedom means
We drink from the same well,

We wade in the same stream,
We stand under the same bell,
We ride the same train.
We stand on the same scale of
Liberty, justice, equality.

Mahalia sings:

Freedom means
The absence of malice,
The presence of charity,
The pursuit of happiness.

Under sun high and moon low,
The children of children announce:

Freedom is moving,
Freedom is gaining speed,
Freedom is advancing to include you and me.

Lincoln, Douglass, Truth,
Tubman, Buddy Boy, Evalina,
Banjo Pete, Colonel Shaw respond:

Every day freedom's fare is
Paid in more and more lives.

From the White House, the
Bittersweet music of victory is heard:
Bells a ringin', bells a ringin', justa ringin'.

The South is justa prayin', painin'.
Generals Grant and Lee are negotiating,
Smoothing the edges of
Victory and defeat.

Children playing on supple grass sing:

Bells are ringing, ringing, ringing
The flag of unity is flying, flying.
Victory is proceeding.

This is the day
President Lincoln stands before
A healing nation, his hands held high,

His voice clear, his
Eyes looking to graves,
His soul weighing the scales of democracy.

He speaks:

I'll always hear the children of children singing:
We ain't gonna study war no more.
We ain't gonna study war no more, no more.
Ain't nothing to stop us now.
Ain't nothing that can hurt us now.
We are standing on green grass.
Now as an undivided nation.

Grandfather and Grandmother rejoice, saying:

The children are picking up sticks,
Kicking cans, playing hide and seek,
Celebrating, enjoying
Gooseberry, blueberry, blackberry pies.

Lilacs touch their lips
When they look at the midnight sun
They remember the dead.

Ancestors call to the children of children:

Remember,
Hate consumes,
Revenge can't live,
Anger's embers turn to flames.

Remember the dead;
Ain't no sacred ground that's unsound.
We are bound to the nation's promise of
Forty acres and a mule.

In front of the nation's pay window,
Wrapped in the red, white and blue,
The children of children stand
Holding the nation's promise.

Year after year while waiting,
Over their heads,
Crows sing the song of a broken promise.

The children of children ask:

Is it safe to stand
Under liberty's cracked bell?
Will the promise we hold be paid?
Will the nation honor its guarantee?

Liberty's cracked bell peals:

In spite of the crack, my ring can be true.
There's no crack in freedom that can't be fixed.
A Lady called Rosa is God's designated fixer.
Every day she sits and waits listening to my ring.

And every day Blacks,
Holding the nation's promise, continue to
Embrace the red, white and blue.

Below the earth,
Seedlings push to sprout.
Believing the promise,
Blacks push to find the nation's cashier.

Ancestors celebrate:

Bells a ringing, ringing, ringing,
Trains a clacking, clacking, clacking.
Drums a beating, beating, beating,
Feet a tapping, tapping, tapping,
Horns a blowing, blowing, blowing,
Hands a clapping, clapping, clapping.
Freedom a rapping, rapping, rapping.

Calli of the valley smiles, singing:

Ain't nothing can turn me and you around.
Ain't nothing that can keep us
From hearing freedom's sound.

Now that we are unbound, we are free.
On new solid ground,
Nothing can turn us around.

We remember the dead.

Responding to their ancestors,
The children of children chant:
Vigilance, vigilance is our creed.
The unexpected can come at any time.
It can come without making a sound.
Vigilance means keeping
Freedom's bells a ringin', ringin'.

Vigilance when confronted means,
Ain't no fact too unimportant to ignore,
Ain't no mind too small, nor too closed
To shout, Hallelujah, Hallelujah.

The children of children sing:

Ain't no doubt too profound to turn back,
Ain't no back too turned that can't confront,
Ain't no resolve that can't be turned,
Ain't no love too buried that can't be found.

The nation's children, dressed in white, are
Holding lilacs; they are honoring the dead.
They say:

Lilacs are our favorite flower.

After paying homage to the dead,
Under a lowering sun, Blacks are
Cautiously crisscrossing the country.

Still waiting, they hear the muffled drumroll,
The lone bugler singing taps.
They see lowered eyes.

Before the creeping train, draped in black,
Inching across the nation's plains,
Weeping Blacks and Whites
Cry their plaintive song:

President Lincoln is . . . Dead.
Add one more.

Buried below the green grass,
America counts the dead.
Remember the dead.
God bless those who died to keep us free.

Their hands clap,
Their feet stomp,
Their emotions spill.
Black people are telling their story.

Rap-rap-rap-rap,
They are recording their journey.
Clickety-clack-clickety-clack,
They are riding trains.
Tap-tap-tap-tap-tap,
They are sharpening awareness.

Under the stars and stripes,
Citizens call:

Today, our flag of unity flies free,
Today, our feet walk without shackles,
Our voices speak above a whisper,
Our once divided families
Gather to wrap their souls
Around yesterday's pain and shame.

Today under a new sun our country begins to heal.
Today Blacks and Whites smell lilacs.

Today mourners hear Walt Whitman's voice.
In yards, front yards and back yards,
He stands and shouts:

Honor the dead.
President Lincoln's spirit lives.

When others are added to the list of the dead,
Muffled bells toll, citizens scold:

Our nation demands,
Stop the killing,
Stop the crows.

In President Lincoln's memory
Seedlings sprout, dull bells peal,
Voices sing:

Remember, no malice, only charity.
Remember, no vengeance, only vigilance.
Remember, no deconstruction, only reconstruction.
Remember, no destruction, only construction.

See, see the country,
See freedom's flag draped over the train
Carrying the body of President Lincoln.
Today we see the train inching, just inching.

The children of children, standing along the tracks
Follow the train carrying
The man called Lincoln. They bow down
And recite:

My country 'tis of thee,
Oh sweet liberty,
Sweet, sweet liberty.

It's me, Black Tiny Shiny,
It's me, Banjo Pete,
It's me, Colonel Shaw,
It's me, See See Rider.

It's us, the men of the 54th,
It's all who died at Fort Pillow,
Remembering the dead.

The nation is singing,
Praying, healing,
Pealing, appealing.

The nation is kneeling before God,
Holding Old Glory,
Telling the sweet, old story of
Rebirth:
Of unity, liberty, equality, in our country.

The united nation calls:

Do you see what we see?
Do you hear what we hear?
Do you feel the bells vibrating, calling,
Just fashioning a new day?

The children of children join
The multitude of new citizens to sing:

No more fighting, killing.
No more will Blacks be
Outside freedom's shore.
We answer the bell of awareness.
We demand equality for
Citizens of all colors.

We hear Americans mingling
Down by the riverside,
Where all bathe in new knowledge.
It's the place where
There is only the human race;
The place where equality
Is always in a state of fuller grace.

It's the place where the nation hears:

No more. No more.
No more will Jim Crow
And his crows darken America's sky.
No more Black Code, fugitive laws.

We've turned from slaving,
We've turned from injustice,
To removing the mask of crows,
To knowing the strength of our resolve.

Down by the riverside,
We wash our hands.

Hands that
Rowed, hoed, chopped,
Pulled, towed, smashed.
Hands that carry facts,
Crack, snap,
Turn pages.

Hands that
Now evaluate, delegate,
Notate and rotate,
Write legislation for Reconstruction,
Write legislation for the Freedman's Bank.

Hands that tie,
Invite, incite, unite.
Our hands fix and mix,
Build, and polish,
Support, sow, lay new tracks.
Our hands
Tenderly take care of
Lilacs swaying free under
The Stars and Stripes.
Our hands expertly hold,
Anoint, baptize.

Our hands never tire.
They wrap, and when
They write, create, and score
They measure, they keep perfect time.

Down by the riverside where flowers grow
Where birds nest, where children play, where
Hands lock around Prometheus's light,
They hold precious the gift of life,
The gift of recording the songs of the soul,
The gift to appreciate the inchworm,
The soaring eagle, a copper sun,

Hot buttered beans, dancing flowers,
The gift to acknowledge
The next moment is the most precious.

The hands of
Evalina, Buddy Boy, Maudell Sleet.
Banjo Pete and Running Boy
Clear the way for the children of children.

Before boarding they declare:

We know the promise of a note
From years of holding a broken note
We learn to blend harmony and melody
To the lyrics of life,
To half notes, eighth notes,
To whole and quarter notes,
To broken flatted notes.

After composing, arranging,
Playing and performing,
We use notes in
Themes and musical schemes.

Before cashing them
We make sure all notes
Deliver their maximum value.

No more, no more will we accept
Payment in broken notes.

Evalina and Banjo Pete sing:

No more slavin,'
No more cowerin',
Grovelin', no more holding on to
Useless notes.

Before Buddy Boy tightens a new belt around
His waist, he tells the children of children:

We are rising to meet a new dawn,
We bathe in insight.
We will sit with Rosa Parks
Through the stormy night.

Three sisters, Insight, Awareness, Understanding,
Daughters of Mother Awareness and See See Rider
Recite:

This light, shining bright
Is for you and you.
See it. Feel it.
It's not hard to find.
Find it, hold it, protect it.
Our soul's light shines, shines, shines;
The country is gonna be just, just fine.

Under sun high and moon low
The light of hope and faith is passed.
Buddy Boy gives it to

Sojourner Truth

Tiny Shiny who gives it to Sojourner Truth
Who gives it to the wind
That settles in parks.

Black and White receivers of the bright light
Rejoice, saying:

Shine, shine, shine.
Let this light shine,
Shine for those who follow,
Gather round.
The light that shines leaves no one behind.

Children holding flowers
Playing drums, speaking in tongues.
Preening and prancing, passing,
Learning, evaluating, digesting,
Build support for a more
Inclusive democracy.

Shining, the children of children cross
Selma's bridge.
On buses in Montgomery, Alabama.
They push to ride in unrestricted seats . . .
They wait for Rosa Parks.

The children of children gather
At the mall in Washington, D.C.,
At lunch counters throughout the nation,
On public transportation they

Begin to use their might,
To gain what's right.

The children of children
Carry the weak.
They open jails.
Like Rosa Parks they refuse to move.

With the sun in her face,
And the wind carrying the message,
Ruth Brown calls:

Lord, Lord, Lord,
We thank you for taking our hands.
Leading us to the Promised Land.

The children of children listen
To the voice of wisdom:

Learning:
Learning swells, sweetens,
Peals, peels.
Learning empowers.

With crows flocking and cawing overhead,
The children of children hear:

This is Ku Klux Klan's land.
Our anthem:
Run, nigger, run.

Harriet Tubman

Burn, nigger, burn.

The children of children demand:

Let my people go.
Let my people out of
The oppression of Dixieland.

Black people break shackles,
In schools they swim deeper,
Run faster.
They learn to avoid harm.

In bands they come playing, performing.
They come marching and fighting the Klan.
Now, they come dressed in knowledge;
They come singing:

Blue birds fly,
Bees suckle;
We will not hide,
We advance in pride.

From far and near, crows yell:

We'll never let niggers go to the river.

Voices call:

Let Black people go.

Day after day
Ruth Brown, Evalina, Buddy Boy,
Banjo Pete, Ma Rainey, are
Getting stronger, wiser,
Mourning with the
Blood of our murdered people.

We join John Henry hammering.
Together we strike, speaking:

By and by, we'll go beyond
The river.
We'll stand in the
Middle of equality's vast green lawn.
We'll share in all the fruits
Of freedom and democracy.

Down by the riverside we'll sing:

No more, no more dragging, chaining
No more breaking us like oxen,
No more murdering,
No more blocking our way to the river.

Harriet Tubman's back is turned,
Her feet sink deep in mud.
Even when crows bump against her
She calls:

My people must be free.

Jim Crow chants:

For those seeking equality, justice,
Unrestricted liberty like whites
The Black Code rules this country.
If you come this way
You'll never see, nor feel the sun again.

If you fight,
We'll hang more than a few.
Harriet, that includes you.

From under a sky of blue.
Look! Look!
Point those with a different view.

Magpies and jackdaws and blue jays,
Robins, and colorful woodpeckers with Harriet
Lead the children of children
From the troubled land.

Calli sings:

Gold spills over them
When the human train is coming through the sun,
When birds sing, when schools of fish swim,
When flowers sway,
When the children of children frolic in sweet grass,
When they drink sweet water from deeper wells.
When serious students climb higher
When enlightenment shines.

Down by the riverside
All bathe in the light of knowledge.
All stand enjoying Gabriel playing:

Come and build down by the riverside
Where hands bathe in a healing mist.

Ancestors harmonize:

Someday we's gonna march,
March on Washington, D.C.
Lord, Lord, Lord, on that day with
Giants leading,
We'll hear Gabriel playing.
Justa calling, just welcoming all
To take our hand.

Guide us.
Lord, just guide us
Over this land.
Lord, we are making our stand.

America is the land of liberty,
The land of the free.

The children of children sing:

Our brother, See See Rider,
Sees everything.

When his daughter, Sister Awareness, joins him
At the well they sing:

Ida B. Wells and Mahalia Jackson
Are gone. Gone on,
Down the tracks.
They won't come back.

We shape a new refrain.
The Black Code must end.

We link hands praying:

Precious Lord, help us,
Lead us. Lord, come this way.
The Black Code must end.

Under sun high and moon low,
The children of children come in droves.
They drink from Ida B. Wells's wells.
They sing with Mahalia Jackson.

They come from schools,
Using better tools.

The children of children chant:

The deeper the well,
The fresher the water,
The bigger the cup,

The larger the number
Who drink.

Every day we visit the sisters:
Insight, Awareness, Understanding.
We learn their support is like steel.

Across the land children instruct:

Mother, Father, come this way
The doors to schools,
To pools are open,
Don't look back.

See See Rider is waiting,
He's pointing to those learning.

Mother, Ida and Mahalia are telling us:

Before long we'll be drinking from the
Nation's deepest wells.
We drink longer
We swim and climb farther.
We move from the fringe
To the center of green lawns.

Parents fill our cups with
More than clear water.
They fill them with ideas
That strengthen
Awareness, insight, understanding.

Under sun high and moon low,
Dressed in black, hair tied in a bun.
Mahalia Jackson sings:

Never will our bags be empty again.

The power of President Lincoln's will
Holds the nation.
He's stretching, justa stretching.

The nation sees two flags,
One with the X of the Confederacy.
One with stripes, with blue, and white stars.
One stands for separation,
One stands for one nation.

Voices cry:

Never two separate flags.
Never, never two flags,
Unfurling, curling, dividing.
Under one flag,
The declaration resounds,
Our country is no longer splitting, splintering.

General Grant has moved through Georgia.
General Lee is defeated.
The Stars and Stripes wave
Day and night.
The bell of unity tolls;
The Civil War is over.

part two

Jubilee

The bright voice of America cries:

Nothing else will do
Liberty, Justice, Equality,
Support you, you, you, and me

This is the time
To accept the nation's promise
Of forty acres and a mule
This is the time to explore the lawns
Beyond the river

Under ringing bells
Rejoicing souls shout:

Is this the day?
Is this the day to ring our bell?
To enjoy victory's inclusive beat.
Good God almighty, Is this the time?

Let us pray:

Tall is the cypress,
Strong is the oak.
Both need rest.
Lord, slavin' tests!
Lord, slavin' tests!

Free! Free! We's Free!
Nothing more. Freedom is best.

Great day in the morning.
We's Free.

Everywhere bells are justa ringing.
Feet are dancing, hearts are throbbing,
Mothers are hugging, faces are smiling,
Brothers and sisters are parading.

The nation calls:

Freedom is here.
The war is over,
The nation is united.

Over the country
The stench of war is dissipating.
People are praying, giving thanks.
People are planning, preparing,
Settling, joining, beginning.

Eyes once closed in horror and sorrow,
Now brim with relief.
Eyes of the freed now gleam
With the promise of belief.

Pride is in eyes,
Praise lives in the vigilant.
Songs are sung.
Freedom's bell tolls.

Morning, noon, and night,
Tolling bells brighten
The wayward, the wary, the beaten warriors.

Yesterday's pain, cruelty, bitterness,
Yield to optimism, enthusiasm.

The children of children
Dance and sing, asking:

Who owns the sun, moon, and stars?
Who colors the night with dreams?
Who corrects wrongs?
Who sees what we see?

Who's stronger than a prayer?
Who owns the ground
That holds the dead?
Who will sit facing crows,
With the lady on the bus?

Is this gettin' down day?

Under an arching rainbow,
Small children, on green lawns,
Playing kick the can sing:

We fill our bags in the sun;
Freedom for us has just begun.

Sho 'nuff, we count.
We add, subtract, multiply.
We keep an accurate score.
Sho 'nuff
We fill our bags
With more and more.

We weigh facts, exercise judgment,
We render thoughtful decisions,
We work, walk, accomplish,
We pull our own weight.

The children of children recite:

We love stars in the sky
We love dawn's new light.
We love all through the night.

Time brings change.
We arrange, compose,
We make room for all.

Leaves turn green,
The moon is bright,
Flowers are in bloom,
Democracy makes room.

Sista Understanding calls:

No more massa,
No more ships,

No more knucklin' under
The massa's whips.
No more Black cargo
Spoon-filling ships.

No more, no more,
No more slavin' in
Cane, tobacco, cotton fields.
No more pain.
No more shame.
Today's work is for personal gain.

Crows are murderers;
Their anthem:

Kill niggas.
Murder, murder, murder,
Lynch, tar, and feather,
Burn, shoot, discriminate,
Segregate.

Crows caw:

Niggas, they's no account.

Murders increase,
Shallow, unmarked graves grow,
Horror settles,
Weary Blacks yell:

Stop the crows.

The children of children hear
Grandfather and Grandmother's
Plaintive song:

Stay away from crows.
Crows bring carnage,
Crows deprive, devastate,
Crows disembowel our people.

Grandmother and Grandfather instruct:

Pick your own crop
Get your forty acres and a mule.
Allow no one
To take your bags
With promises of pay.

Fill your own bags,
Carry them.
Weigh them.
Count them.
Mark, tie, pile them.

Although times are austere,
Don't despair.
What you achieve is your fare.

Ancestors' voices rise, saying:

Help will come
From those fillin' bales
From those leavin' slavery's jails.

Relieved mothers and fathers shout:

Look at Buddy Boy's
Head a bobbin',
Justa bobbin', bobbin'.
He's walkin' with the great man,
Justa walkin' with pride.
They's walkin' stride for stride.
Frederick Douglass is his guide.

Buddy Boy asks:

When you ran away
Did you travel by day?
Did you hide in the hay?
When you caught Freedom's train
Did you have a secret way?
Did you pray every day?

Did you use a guide who was wise?
Did you wear a disguise?
Did you ever hear our ancestors cry?

All across the nation
The children are watching
The giant statesman and boy

Unfurl the red, white and blue.
That's when they begin to level
The steep grade of uneven spotted lawns.

The Stars and Stripes waves
Its approval.
Frederick Douglass speaks:

Freedom is for all.
Freedom, like healthy grass,
Is best when it endures, extends,
And blends.

Democracy is of the people,
By the people, for the people.
It cannot restrict one race
And advance another.
It cannot favor one creed, religion,
One political persuasion over another.

Freedom's single point of view
Is to enhance the color
Of the green lawns of democracy.
Freedom must treat all citizens the same.

From the United States Supreme Court
Salmon P. Chase, justice-conductor,
On Freedom's train, calls:

All aboard,
Come out of nooks,

Come out of crannies.
This train is for you.

Come, we're crossing land
Once held by the Ku Klux Klan.
Now, the Court is assuring a democratic plan.

Clickety, clickety, clack, clack.
The soil is red.
Freedom riders on Freedom's trains
Crossed the valley of the dead.
Without fear, on bare feet,
They cross
Poppy fields filled with thorns.

Frederick Douglass says:

You have the same human rights
As the man from Springfield, Illinois,
Wearing the top hat.

Frederick Douglass points to the ground, saying:

Gettysburg will live long in our history.

From the grandstand Lincoln said:

Four score and seven years ago
Our fathers brought forth . . .

In one voice
The children of children
Standing with Buddy Boy, ask:

Do you hear?
Did you hear?
Freedom is for all.

Frederick Douglass speaks:

We have a new nation,
A united nation,
A healing nation,
A multiracial nation.

It's for all of us to know
The meaning of democracy,
The value of liberty,
The fairness of opportunity,
The weight of justice,
The purity of the scale measuring equality.

Never forget the cost:
Souls maimed,
Dreams shattered,
Lives lost.

It's up to you, my fellow citizens,
To never let freedom grow cold,
To never let it grow old.

Keep liberty's bell tolling.

Protect it.

Drink from its wells.

Remember what President Lincoln died for:

One God.

One government.

One flag.

One commitment.

One people.

President Lincoln, in a voice

Heard throughout the nation

Called for unity of our land.

Unity means coming together

To share,

In the middle of green lawns,

Hot apple pie, fresh milk.

All must enjoy freedom and the

Fullness of democracy.

At the time, Frederick Douglass told President Lincoln:

This is a time

To correct injustice,

To remove nesting crows,

To strengthen Reconstruction,

To remove all racial barriers.

This is a time
To kill the dogma of Jim Crow,
To nullify the Black Code.

Rights cannot be measured;
Black rights, White rights
Emit the same light.

Freedom is owned by the nation.
The nation is owned by you and me.
Its responsibility is the same to me
As it is to you.

Democracy is of the people,
By the people, for the people.

It cannot restrict one and advance another.
It cannot be concerned with
Only one race, one creed, one religion,
One political dogma.
It has no single point of view.

Its view is not just for the privileged,
Or the knowledgeable few.

What's claimed for me
Is claimed for you.
All ride the same train
Clickety, clickety, clack, clack.

Answer the call,
This train is for all,
Clickety, clickety, clack, clack.

The Supreme Court speaks:

No, Billy Boy,
No, Banjo Pete,
No, Evalina,
No, Black Tiny Shiny,
You do not have to steal away.

Rights grow like ripples,
They cannot crest or splash,
They cannot fade.
They stand tall.

Rights run to tributaries,
To brooks and ponds,
Lakes and streams.

They run to all citizens
There's no reason
For the Mason-Dixon Line
To draw a line
Between color, religion, creed, race.

Conductor Salmon Chase
Of the Supreme Court calls:

All aboard!
On Freedom's Trains,
Rights gather steam.
They widen, they bridge,
They expand, they demand.
They have the power to command.
Freedom's trains support Blacks' rights.

Get on board,
Hoist the red, white and blue.

Come climbing, come rowing,
Come singing, come bridging,
Come mending, come correcting.

Come connecting, come replacing,
Come shining, growing, drinking,
Come swimming, swinging, thinking,
Come jamming,
Just come as you are . . . just come.

From the steps of the country's
Highest court of Justice,
A tall black lady with a compelling voice,
Marian Anderson, sings:

Remember John Brown.

While fighting to end slavery he preached:
Freedom is for Black and White.

John Brown's spirit fans the
Intense flames of freedom.
There is no shame in freedom's flame.

When John Brown
Sees Douglass separating from him,
He smiles, saying:

At night, out of sight,
Frederick Douglass does
His best work.

Bells ring, bells sing.
Bags fill with the alphabet of
F-r-e-e-d-o-m.
Banners wave.
The colors of passion heat the sun.

The children of children call:

We got more than one bag.
We got bags that say
We's Free! Free! Free!

No more bossman with a whip, whipping us.
Got to enlighten those who do not understand.
Got to make a glorious sound.
We's Free! Free! Free!

The children of children sing:

Today, we weep no more, no more.
Today, we ford the Jordan.
Today, liberty's door opens.
Today, we bathe down by the riverside.

Today, Marcus Garvey stands talking,
Leading, parading.
Developing, advancing.

His followers sing:

With freedom on our side
We can't fail.
Nothing can stop freedom now.

The children of children see their giants:

Garvey, DuBois, Booker T., Tubman, Truth,
Standing near the green lawns of democracy.

While facing a new sunrise they chant:

Truth needs no cover,
In time there will be no
Mason-Dixon Line,
No line between
Color, religion, creed, or race.

The nation hears
Marcus Garvey's father's chant:

This day,
Under the midnight sun,
I hold Marcus, my son,
Up to you.

I am, I am the son of a Black man.
Marcus, my son, will stand above the crowd.
He will fish from the edge of exasperation
With the string of experience.

Under sun high and moon low,
He'll work to
Strengthen our resolve,
Temper our Intelligence,
Attend the unattended,
Raise ideas to the sky.

Marcus will keep time
For more than
DuBois's "Talented Tenth."
He will be the man keeping time
For Black people of all kinds.

Under a sunlit sky of blue,
In perfect marching time,
Marcus, the son of a Black man,
Leads the parade across 125th Street,
To stand in Apollo's light.

In uniforms, his followers
Glide as one unified tide.

Marcus, the son of a Black man, sings:

We must blend differences,
Tighten what we share in common.
We must always appear as one,
In body, in spirit, in soul.

We must hear the lady called
Lordy, Lordy, Miss Claudy.
Circling round and round them,
She calls:

I don't understand you three sons,
Booker T., DuBois, Garvey.
Why don't you get together?
Don't you know you are diffusing our song.

I don't understand
You three giants.
Why don't you get together?
Don't you know you are confusing us,
Weakening our unity?

Lord, Lord, hear me.
I'm Miss Claudy.
Those three just
Grumble, grumble, grumble.

Brothers, it's up to you
To help us sail,
To just keep sailing.

Miss Claudy's strong voice shouts:

Lord, I join with the
Children of children
Who insist that these three leaders:

Stop pointing!
Stop assailing!
Stop failing!
Stop dividing!
We've had enough!
Enough!

Don't they know
All the wheels on Freedom's train
Must pull and roll together?

Don't they know,
The wheels in front,
The wheels in the middle,
The wheels in back
Must sing the same song?

Clickety, clickety, clack, clack
Clickety, clickety, clack, clack

With the children of children circling her,
Miss Claudy points, saying:

Wheels going in the
Same direction enhance
Power and performance.
Together they cover a greater distance.
Unity turns away an unexpected attack.

There's room
For Booker T.,
For DuBois,
For Garvey,
For all three to agree,
To bend their knees in togetherness.
There's room for you three giants
To shape and forge,
To begin to share the same paper,
To help turn each other's pages.

They welcome sisters,
Phillis Wheatlcy and Sista Awareness,
Who join them.

Under sun high and moon low
Sista Wheatley instructs:

No more will the brothers be separated,
No more, no more, no more.

No more America in mournful strains,
No more wrongs and grievances tolerated.

No more. No more
Will we be rootless in America.
Never forget we are one, one people,
One in purpose.

A letter comes to Sister Phillis Wheatley:

Thank you most sincerely
For your polite notice of me.
Your style and manner exhibit
Proof of your talent.
I'm pleased you think well of me,
President George Washington.

With ease and insight,
Phillis places the letter alongside
The Declaration of Independence,
And the nation's promissory note.

Over the sound of the train gathering speed,
Clickety, clickety, clack
She calls:

Get on board,
DuBois, Booker T., Garvey.
Even though I lived before you,
I'm with you.
Your gift now is to lead.

Your fathers are holding
You up to the golden sun.

John Brown

Lead, unite, meld, shine.
Your gift now is to lead!

Your mission is to
Destroy the Black Code,
Destroy Jim Crow and his crows,
Destroy the fugitive laws!

We know with you leading
No burning cross,
No simmering embers,
No field of smoke
Will harm us.

A father holding a baby over his head sings:

I'm the son of a Black man.
I offer my son, asking you to
Keep him
Safe from a gun.
Keep him
Safe from trouble.
Keep him
Safe from Jim Crow's crows.

God, let my son gleam in silver and gold.
Let him dream.
Let him sit under an apple tree.
Let him row from shore to shore,
Enjoying the fruits of liberty and democracy.

Standing hand in hand,
Phillis Wheatley and Sister Awareness sing:

Out of clickety clack,
Out of rap-rap-rap,
Out of clap-clap-clap,
Out of pat-pat-pat,
Comes the music of our people.

See them rapping,
See their hands clapping,
See their minds keeping
Time with the clickety clacking.

See them creating under a silver moon.
On lawns hear them dancing in
The purity of new rain.
See them tasting the warmth of family love.
See them paying homage to those
Breaking barriers, opening new territories.

Hear the sip, sip, sip
Of them drinking from deepening
Democratic wells.

Hear the tick, tick, tick,
The sound of Lemuel Haynes at Concord,
Leading a band of minutemen.

Tap, tap, tap is the pen
Of Benjamin Banneker

Planning, designing
Washington, D.C.

Get on board
From the voice
Of Jean Baptiste Pointe DuSable.
Dig, dig, dig is the sound of his shovel
Birthing Chicago.

Joining the train as conductors,
Whose wheels are rollin',
Justa rollin' are:
Freedom fighters:
James Armistead,
Cinque, Nat Turner,
John Brown.

From a brown spot of grass
We hear a mother telling her child:

Child, change is coming,
It's coming, justa coming,
Freedom done brought a change.
It has stopped raining in Georgia, in
Shout It Out, Tennessee.

Passengers on Conductor Wheatley's train
Intone:

United as families, we ride.
We just ride, ride, ride,

We rejoice, calling.
Board this train,
Rollin' down shiny new tracks.
Get on board, right now!

Never, never will
This train, Freedom's train
Fail or yield
To the men in robes and hoods.
Never will we, the children of children,
Believe Jim Crow and his crows.

They make false deals.
Donning their attire, they hide in woods.
They shoot, they tar and feather Blacks.
They kill, kill, kill.

Voices of our giants,
Past and present, instruct:

It is time for us to untie knots,
To slash the chains that bound
Us to slavery.
It's time to remove the crimson shame
Of slavery.
It's time to sculpt to perfect
Ochre, bronze
To burnish a world full of different hues.

It's time to turn topsoil,
It's a time to pick wild cherries,
It's time to climb sycamores.

With books in hand, pubescent
Schoolgirls listen to
Their teacher, Prudence Crandall:

It's a time to encourage beginners,
Beginners I teach.

Crows, with torches,
Burned my school to the ground.
They can't stop my girls from learning, achieving.
School is more than brick, board, and mortar.

Sitting under an old oak tree,
The class of proud Black girls
Hears Prudence Crandall reciting:

Crows are always determined
To hold Blacks back;
No reading,
No schooling,
No advancing.

From deep in the night,
The girls call back:

Nothing can keep us from learning.
Nothing can keep us from Prudence Crandall's light.

The chorus calls to Crandall's girls:

Crows, crows are everywhere.
They hide in white sheets and hoods.
They dress in suits of respectability.
They have nests
In the foundation of democracy.

Lord, we are aware
Of their cawing.
We pay attention to their coops
In important places.
Wearing smiling faces,
They come dressed in disguises
To gain advantage over
The children of children.

Crows are experts in ambiguous phrases,
Experts in deception,
Experts in conniving.
They come bringing promissory notes,
They come with an agenda to deny
The children of children
Liberty, Justice, Citizenship.

The children of children sing:

This we know:
Soon the protection by federal troops
Is removed from the South.
Soon Nathan Forrest's vicious crows are let loose.

Soon the promise of independence and freedom is broken,
Soon the boon of forty acres and a mule is gone.
Soon thunder rumbles,
Soon dreams are dashed.

Soon the Confederate flag flies high over the defeated.
Soon torsos and tarred bodies swing high from trees.
Soon arm and leg stumps appear.
Soon the shot brings despair.

The shot:
President Lincoln is dead.
Plaintive voices call:

Where are you, Lord?
Soon the scream:
Lord, how can this be?
No! No! Not that!

From down home
On the Yazoo River, Bluesmen sing:

Take away our sins, untangle
Our knotted sorrow.
Take our sins away,
Give us grace.

From deltas, from bayous
The Blues sing:

Save our souls.
Save the nation's soul.
Oh! Sweet liberty, we seek thee,
We honor thee.

This land of Liberty, this land of
Justice and Equality
Belongs to you and me.

Three brothers,
Intelligence, Intellect, Wisdom,
Push to the front of the children of children,
Who are standing before the nation.

They warn:

Jim Crow is a master of the night;
His crows are everywhere.
They nest on the roof of the White House.
They nest in
City, State, and Federal Government.

The voice of Sista Awareness joins in,
Exclaiming:

The lies of crows undermine.
When shooed they coo, seducing
Andrew Johnson, who feeds them.
The president restores them to power.

He gives back their land lost in the war; he
Grants them States' Rights,
Unmonitored and unlimited power
Over Black people.

Dancing under the hanging tree,
The crows boast:

The jiggaboos
Never had a chance.
We leave them on display;
Hanging niggers dance for us.

Nathan Forrest, the leader of all the
Crows, hears the children of children
Telling the nation:

From nest to nest,
From branch to branch
Crows perched on thin limbs
Proclaim their racist policies are right.
We's right 'cause we's white.

The children of children point calling:

Look! Look!
Sista Awareness is exclaiming:
President Andrew Johnson is
Yielding.

Under the protection of President
Andrew Johnson, they boast:

Nigga, stand back.
Nigga, get back.

Armed with the blessing of federal backing
And states' rights, Jim Crow and his crows
Exercise their unrestricted might,
Murdering day and night
Blacks who cross their sight.

Crows yell:

Nigga, get back
Before you're placed on a rack.
Nigga, you better stand back.

Under sun high and moon low
The children of children call:

Crows are clods, bullies,
Cops, judges, lawyers,
Farmers, salesmen, thieves,
Teachers, drivers, dividers.

Crows are everywhere:
Writers, bankers, insurers,
Congressmen, senators, assemblymen,
Governors, mayors, councilmen, officials.

Crows are haters,
Soldiers, informers,
Farmers, travelers,
Planters, liars,
Lynchers, killers.

Under sun high and moon low,
The children of children
United to fight the crows,
Listen to elders who say:

Jim Crow must be stopped.

From the podium, three maturing giants,
Carter Woodson, Walter White, Roy Wilkins
Instruct:

Close ranks and advance.
Gather, gather together.
Don't be afraid.
Gather day and night.
Exercise patience,
Gather new insight.

Democracy is by the people, for the people.
No form of government, however carefully devised,
No principles, no matter how sound,
Will protect the rights of people,
Unless they are faithful to its promise to the governed.

Children of children call:

We will never let the crows damage our faith.
When crows build new nests,
We, the children of children,
Pass harder and harder tests.

Standing on firm land
Is the giant called Divine, Father Divine.
The children of children hear him preach:

I'm God's man.

Approaching Father Divine in a long black robe is
Daddy Grace, another giant of God.
Father Divine and Daddy Grace
Together they divine and say grace:

Our country, 'tis of thee
There is room in this country
For more than you and me;
Rooms that open
To Whites and Blacks,
To Browns and Yellows,
To Reds and Tans.

Marching on greening lawns,
The children of children demand:

Make room for
Bessie Smith and Ma Rainey,

Mahalia Jackson and Marian Anderson,
Billie Holiday and an orphan, named Winfree.

The orphan with the riveting personality
Brings together sisters:
Awareness, Understanding, and Insight,
Maudell Sleet, Angela, and Sojourner Truth,
Harriet Tubman,
Mothers and aunts,
Grandmothers and great-grandmothers,
Drinking sweet water from
Ida B. Wells's deepening wells.

Hear us!
We are one.
Hear!

I am, I am,
I am a Black woman.
In my womb I hold
The gift of tomorrow.
Sons and daughters,
Brothers and sisters,
I am a Black woman
Who carries the seeds.
I am a Black woman
Who digs, prunes,
Plants, harvests.
I am a Black woman
Who comes early and stays late.
I am a Black woman

Who won't allow the
Klan to seal my fate.

I am, I am, I am a Black woman
Who walks unafraid across Dixieland.
The sticks and stones I carry
Make a home, something,
I say, something I own.

I am a Black woman
Who sings lullabies,
Who refuses to say good-bye,
Who looks to the sky,
Who asks, Lord, Lord,
Why? Why? Why?

Will the message, your message, come by and by?
Will you stand with me against the Klan?
Will your light surround my swelling belly with delight?
Will you ride the tide with me?
Together will we set the Klan aside?

I am a Black woman of courage, of faith.
I turn page after page;
I am always engaged.
Yes! I am a Black woman,
I lead, stand, share, birth.

My song, a southern song,
I sing while watching ducks and frogs
Glide on silver spines of cresting ripples.

Every day I sing, I sing:
Dig no more graves for the Klan's misdeeds.
Dig no more in the red clay of Georgia.
Run no more from the murdering band
Run no more from the Klan.

I run with the men of the Massachusetts 54th
I run with John Brown, Nat Turner, Douglass, DuBois.
I run with Booker T., with Buddy Boy, Black Tiny Shiny,
I run with See See Rider,
I run with the Underground Railroad.

I am a Black woman
Who will no longer be chained to grief,
Who will fire no more dirges.
I am a Black woman
Who stirs, sings, and rings bells:
Freedom's bell, liberty's bell,
Democracy's bell.

I drink long,
I drink deep,
I drink until I'm satisfied.
I am, I am a rivulet flowing to greater rivers,
I run through towns, cities and hamlets.

I am a Black woman
Who plays music for the silent.
I tend to the earth.
I declare for you, you, and you,
I ford troubled water,

I will not go aground.
I will not be turned around.

This ground,
This blood-soaked ground,
Is our ground.
I'll never surrender it.
To the Klan.
I am a Black woman
I stand with my man.

I'm called Margaret Walker.
"I sing for my people."
I hear their bittersweet music.
Of grief and belief.

I hear the Blues singer joining
Music makers.
I see my people refusing
To bow to the crows.

I am, I am a Black woman.

I say:
Walk a little faster,
Wade a little deeper,
Hold my hand tighter.
Swim a little farther.
Follow me,
I know the way.

Women, Black women,
Stand, proclaiming,
I am, I am a Black woman.
I stand with giants:
Zora Neale Hurston, Ida B. Wells,
The Walker sisters,
Alice, Margaret, Madam Walker.

I stand with Toni Morrison,
Tubman, Truth,
Evalina, Maudell Sleet, Winfree,
Knowing soon we'll really be free.

I am a Black woman
Who knows what must be done.
For years I've kneaded,
Kneaded worry, kneaded patience.
I've kneaded maiming,
I've kneaded death.
I've kneaded minutes into hours,
Into a life of hope, faith.
I've kneaded misery into another day of belief.
I've kneaded from storm to storm.
I've kneaded what has to be done.

I am the Black woman, the mother of
The children of children,
Who keep
Turning, dreaming,
Learning and advancing.

I am a woman of faith.
I hail from Lookout Mountain.
I climb the summit of Kilimanjaro.
I cross the Nile.
I bathe in the Jordan.

I hunt with my man.
Together we birth a new generation.
In my loins I hold the seeds of royalty,
The promise of tomorrow's giants.
I share my milk,
The milk of life.
Through me, a Black woman,
God presents the gift of life.

Every day I mix fresh pigments.
Every day I paint life bright.

Freedom walks with me,
It talks with me.
It travels on many feet,
On four feet, three feet, two feet,
On one foot.

Yes! I am a Black woman.
My roots go deep,
They go far, they go wide.
No container is big enough,
Deep enough, wide enough, strong enough
To hold the force of liberty, justice, equality,
To hold the force of my growing family.

Hear my echo:

I am the Black woman
Who never looks back,
Who spins and says, come share,
Share apples, strawberries, peaches, melons.
Color my arms, color my lips
With the sweetness of brown
Honey. Seal my lips with
Honeysuckle, with cured love.

Color me woman.
Color me Black.
Color me faithful, hopeful.
Color me determined, loving.
Color my devotion eternal.
Color me mother earth.

From the earth I come,
To the earth my soul's seeds return.

I am a proud Black woman
Married to a Black man.
We are one; nothing can separate us.
Nothing can turn us back from
The rivers, the Nile and the Jordan,
The Mississippi, and the Ohio.

When we stand intertwined
As wife and husband and family,
No lens can distort our commitment.

I am the Black woman who
Fries apples, sweet corn and chicken.
I fry fish down by the riverside
Where lilacs are always in bloom,
Where black and white birds fly
In a clear sky.

Down by the riverside,
I harvest
Peas and corn,
Tobacco and cotton,
Sugar cane and collard greens.
Down by the riverside
My family moves safely from high
Tide to higher tide.

I am the Black woman.
From my belly I birth twins,
Duke Ellington and Billy Strayhorn.
With skill they orchestrate
Black and white notes,
Write new scores,
Arrange and rearrange music.

All over the nation their music is enjoyed.
It harmonizes, it integrates
Melodies, lyrics, and scales.
Scales that cause fingers to pop,
Feet to stomp, hands to clap;

Faces to smile when voices say:

Hit it, swing it, play it.
Play it better, man.
Play your music.
Make it swing all day.

My sons make music that
Enthralls, that
Melds black and white notes creatively, that
Renders listeners spellbound, that
Opens jazzing vistas.

Under sun high and moon low,
The children of children croon:

From the soul of musical giants:
Lester Young, Ben Webster,
Charlie Yardbird Parker,
Louis Armstrong, Miles Davis,
The musical power of Orpheus grows.
Jazz at Birdland captivates
Jim Crow crows.
That leaves them hungry for more and
More soulful music.

The children of children chant:

At Birdland, jazz sirens seduce.
Black and White musicians join
John Coltrane in playing.
The composition of the twins,
Ellington and Strayhorn,

Is the coal-firing,
Fast-moving train called
Modern jazz,
Which sweeps across more
Than the racial plains of America.

Every day the music giants of jazz
Gallop, kick, mix, take flight,
Deliver hot lick after hot lick.

With sons of a Black woman performing,
Music streams and permeates
More than America.
The musical train's whistle blows,
Attracting, announcing, calling,
Telling, conducting.

The giants
Are cookin', just cookin'.

Music lovers shout:

Black birds, Charlie Parker's Yardbirds,
And Jim Crow's crows are flying.
Music has brought them together.

In rhythm Blacks and Whites
Swing, swing, swing.
Winging, singing, swinging.
The music Coltrane is playing is
Blowing, calling, singing, jamming.

The children of children warn:

While giants are creating, and voices are praising,
Justa praising, Jim Crow is waiting.

Look, call the children of children:

Everywhere birds are free, we can
Learn from them.
Witness, Coltrane's playing, his blowing,
His calling, his singing,
His cookin', justa cookin' new music.
People are praising.

James Meredith, the first Black to attend,
Is stepping to swim in the
University of Mississippi's pool.
From the softest grass on the lawns of
Democracy, the children of children
Encourage James Meredith:

Swim deeper, quicker, better
Swim with tenacity, swim harder.

The children of children shout:

Do you hear? He won't miss.
Ole Miss is hissing, just hissing.
Crows dressed as students, as professors, are
Shaking, cawing, jawing, threatening, scheming.

The country is listening, watching
Hiding crows crouching in high grass.
His classmates see James
Standing straight, books tall in his hands,
Walking fast, walking wrapped in faith,
Walking facing hate.

Men in flapping white sheets bark:
Nigra!
Kill! Kill the nigra.
Ya just a smart-ass, no-good nigger boy,
We's gonna tar and feather ya before
Hanging you.

From far and near crows peer, leering,
Searching James for a sign of fear.
Unafraid, James hears
The children of children telling him:

Stay safe, James.
Sit deep and secure in your seat.
Read, listen, study, spread seeds further.
Turn another page, polish
Polish learning.

Martin Luther King's voice bathes
The children of children.
They hear him telling James:

Breathe deep, speak calm,
Make inquiries, retain your faith.

Never permit shadows to put out the light.

With books in one hand and faith in the other,
James faces his mentor, Dr. King,
Who tells him:

The day will come,
When warm hands comfort you,
When the nation's hands support you,
When the doors of Whites-only schools
Open to Blacks.

Your innocence is not temporal.
Your quest is not only of this time.
Your Innocence is like morning dew,
Like laughing, like giggling,
Like Protecting tadpoles, like the mist of spring.

It's like hot baked bread,
It's like chilled apple cider, it's like taking a
First step, it's like reading a book,
It's like holding Mother's hands.

It's thank you, God.
Thank you for
Opening Ole Miss to Blacks.
Thank you for allowing us to be ready
To face the challenge with Rosa Parks,
The challenge of going beyond the river.

When the children of children face
The challenge of the Governors

Of Mississippi, Alabama, Georgia,
South Carolina, North Carolina,
Dr. Martin Luther King speaks:

No lie can tarnish truth.
Demand more from your self.
See more, seek more.
Demand more from professors,
Demand more from the City, the State,
The Federal authorities.

Knowledge is the key.
It unlocks debilitating ignorance,
While expanding power.

Today is a new day.
Today, James Meredith graduates from Ole Miss.

Across the nation, the song of death is sung:

James Chaney, Andrew Goodman, Michael Schwerner
Today, the three have been called.
They know the meaning of death.
Crows murdered them,
Still, we count the dead, still counting the
Dead.

Throughout the country rain spills, the nation grieves.
The rage of the Klan flames grow higher
America listens to the dissonance of death.

In honor of these three brothers
The children of children recite:

There will be no gloomy Sunday,
'Cause Monday is the Blues day,
'Cause Georgia is on our minds,
'Cause someday death comes to all.

The nation's voices blend to pray:

God bless the child, child, child,
John, Andrew, Michael.
James.

We hear them singing:

Rise up, rise up, children,
Rise up and follow
In dat great gittin-up mornin',
Rise up, rise up,
Rise up and follow.

Dr. King states:

Today, and every day, our brothers
Live in our minds, our spirits, our hearts.
Our brothers rest under God's sky,
While Gabriel calls:
Cross over children,
Climb Jacob's ladder,
Rise up, rise up, rise up.

On this day of death,
Only the barren bent trees
Sing their leafless song.

Under sun high and moon low
The children of children call:

Look who's getting on board,
The man called Satchel Paige.
From a mound, unafraid, he throws
A hard white fast ball that mows
Down Jim Crow and his crows.

To get to the man called
Satchel, crows step from dugouts.
From tall grass, crows step out,
Carrying more than broken bats
And tattered gloves.
They step, issuing broken promises;
They step, celebrating burning crosses,
Hanging Black bodies.

Dancing round the mound,
Holding the tarred and feathered,
Crows celebrating call nigger, nigra, nigga,
But their score
Against the giant Satchel is always
Zero, zero, zero.

Opposite the baseball field
Another giant, a crow fighter,

The Brown Bomber steps into the boxing ring.
Crows flock to challenge him.

They hear the bell ring; they face the
Bomber with hands of thunder and
Fists fast as lightning.
No one has ever seen his jab,
No one has ever seen
His killer quick right cross.

Joe Louis's quicksilver hands
Always leave crows sore and unsure.
That's for sure.

Voices cheer when they hear
Joe Louis call to the crows:

There is no ring big enough for crows to hide in.
There is no bell fast enough to stop my power.
You can duck and feint, you can bob and weave.
What you can't do is to hear the sound
That sends you to the ground.

Black and White leaders broadcast:

It's a new season
The weather has changed.
Blackbirds, jackdaws, magpies circle.
Butterflies flutter, bees hum, cicadas sing.
Leaves splash green and flowers gleam:
Gold, purple, yellow, white, red, blue.

Jazzing, Black and White music makers call:

Jamming knows no racial venues.
With ease it colors emotions.
Man, what you're playing is hip.
Don't stop; keep on cooking.

In honky-tonks where jazz jams,
The children of children sing:

Charlie Yardbird Parker's groovin' birds
And Dizzy Gillespie's swinging
White and black notes seduce crows.
The musical giants' agile fingers
Execute the music right side up,
Wrong side down.
And when there's no music to read
They create scores, interposing,
Composing, interpreting, improvising.

Hum-hum-hum,
Bee-bo-beebo-bo,
Be-bop-bop-bop,
They are always on time.
They never play a wrong note.

When grooving, musicians say:

Jazz is personal, universal,
It draws, it enters; it leads the way to
Just beyond the river.

Black and White listeners yell:

Sing it man! Sing it!
Just sing it!
Bird, sing it through your alto sax;
Play it Dizzy, through your trumpet.

We know jazz is the song of the soul
Of the once enslaved.
We hear you creating Anthems, Gospel, Hymns,
The ma and pa Soulful, liberating Blues.
We hear you playing
The "Georgia Cake Walk."

Jazz's swinging riffs spread
Throughout the world; crows
Flock to drink from jazz's creative wells.
Jazz is heard
Jamming across the Klan's land.

From bandstands
Music lovers are thrilled when Black and White
Dancers swing their partners free, saying:

Don't stop now! Set it free! Keep the music
Groovin' from mountaintop
To treetop.

Clapping their hands and stomping their feet
Swingers shout:

Man, it's wonderful, play it sweet, man!
There can be no more music in the air
For you than for me.

Standing, linked arm in arm, the children of children
Dance around trees full of large crows.
The nation hears:

Music, like freedom, belongs to all.
Freedom is the same for all the notes on
A score, musical notes, black notes, white notes,
Half notes, whole notes.

Freedom shouts
The Gospels, Hymns, Jazz and Blues.
The crows cannot compete with
Dizzy and Bird's swinging birds.

Under the rising sun, the children of children
Speak:

The music of birds has a universal appeal.

The children of children say:

Thank God
For eyes to see, for hands to hold wonder,
For a heart full of love, for lips to kiss,
For lips to blow music.

Thank God
For ears to behold, for voices to sing.
For the ability to create;
We give thanks for an understanding mind,
For intelligence, for strength that comes
With a developing intellect.
We thank God for the gift of heaven's glory.

Thank you for
Beauty, for smells that swell,
For breath that brings life
To flutes and horns,
For life to children whose
Legs and feet skip over and under rope.

Thank you for
Hands and fingers to pick up sticks;
For legs to run
Voices that holler, run as fast as you can;
For feet to kick the can.

We, the children of children, know
We must hold the string taut when flying kites.
Every day, all day, we brace our backs and our
Shoulders to the changing winds carrying
Crows throughout the country.

In their souls the children of children know
Faith is to union as hope is to belief,
Sun is to shine as moon is to tide,
Tide is to change as Jim Crow is to night.

The children of children call:

Lord, it's you we thank for
Threads to weave brown, yellow, blue,
Black, white into a multicolored quilt that
Covers the United America.

We thank you for the music makers,
Dizzy and Bird, who tie me to you,
Who create an enjoyable place
To lay our burdens down, a place
Where we can
Wander further, longer, safer.

Under sun high and moon low,
We know:

In a democracy no number means
More to you than to me.
We know all citizens have a number that's
Equal in importance.

No more will you subtract
From me and add only to . . .
Our numbers must agree.

No more will enslavers have the only pencil,
No more will they cook the books,
No more will Jim Crow and
His crows keep the only score.

Under sun high and moon low,
The children of children are
Presenters and pointers.
They incorporate, investigate, and open books.
They carry leaves, build homes,
Gather weeds, fill pockets with
Notions that fulfill and thrill.
They create, they share music,
Music of togetherness.

The children of children's chant
Covers the nation:

As Cain and Abel are brothers,
As solid is to faith,
As blade is to silent,
As yoke is to horse,
As roots are to family.
As Cain and Abel are brothers.

The children of children call:

We must create myths.
Myths fill the space between true and false.
Myths are the way humanity handles
Dreams and reality, dawn and night,
Hope and faith, fable and tale.
The myth of heaven and hell,
The myth of the Children of Children joining giants
To drink cool sweet water

Leads to the well of Congress where
Adam Clayton Powell speaks:

Don't hold on to empty promises,
Like the myth of forty acres and a mule.
Hold on to trust, its thrust goes
Deeper, broader, straighter, higher.

Adam calls:

Baby, baby, baby,
We must always
Keep the faith.
Keep the faith baby.

In the morning when the air is fresh,
In the noon when the sun is bright,
In the evening when twilight shines,
Our soulful giants strut their stuff.

Baby, baby, it's our myth.
Let us present:
Just facts, tight facts.
History joins facts, dreams, imagination to
Sing the song of our
Developing mythology.

Adam Clayton Powell standing
In front of a podium calls:

Faith, truth, and light live in
The Father!
The Son!
The Holy Ghost!

They are in the belief, the promise,
The note, the mule, the forty acres.
They are in the bridges we cross,
The sun, the moon, the air.
They are in the language of honesty,
They are in a day that carries the wind and more . . .

From the heart of Harlem,
Minister Powell preaches:

Remember myth's light is everywhere.
The nation's flag of inclusion is no myth.
Red, white, and blue has its own mythology.
Racial biology cannot color
America's democracy.

From Congress, the man called Adam
Tells the children of children:

Jackie Robinson steps to the plate.
With all his might he strikes a white ball.
With all his might he strikes down barriers.
With all his might he strikes down the color line.
Don't let crows tag Jackie out.

Across America cheering
Black and White crowds chant:

Jackie! Jackie! Jackie
Keep it! Keep the faith.
Your faith is our faith.

The crows scream:

Blackie, Jackie, Black nigger boy,
We gonna kill you and all like you.
You smart-ass, Black nigger;
We gonna hang the likes of you.

From the grandstand,
Adam Clayton Powell calls out:

No matter what you crows do,
We won't drown in faith, truth, and light.
It's no myth the three giants,
Jackie, Satchel, Joe, shine
With Prometheus's light,
With Sisyphus's strength,
With Apollo's speed.

Power lives in the rising sun,
Power lives in understandings,
Power lives in the rustle of green leaves protecting lilacs,
Power lives in waking to loving in the morning,
Power lives in the moment of birth,
Power lives in the spirit of the 54th.

Power lives in the beliefs of Douglass,
Power lives in the wisdom of DuBois,
In the determination of Booker T.,
In the philosophy of Garvey.

Power lives
In the light of Harriet Tubman,
In the truth of Sojourner,
In the advocacy of Ida B. Wells.

Power lives
In real and imaginary giants:
Tiny Shiny, Banjo Pete,
Maudell Sleet, Evalina,
Angela, Brown, Buddy Boy, Anderson,
Robeson, Wolf, Rainey.

Power lives
In our united embrace of
Amber waves of grain,
In the Stars and Stripes,
In the myths we draw.

The children of children respond:

It's time to grow wiser, stronger, smarter.
It's time to attack ignorance.
It's time to rub enlightment until it glistens and
We own it!
It's time to know no wave is too short to ripple.

This day, when facing yowling, snapping dogs,
Hope is heard in the voice of Lady Day,
Hope swells in the song
Mahalia Jackson sings:

Precious Lord, take our hand,
Take us over the bridge.

Hope swings with Sarah Vaughan
When she calls:

Misty eyes are not here today.
We have come to cross Selma's bridge.
No day will we give way to
Bull Connor and his mad biting dogs.
Hope is fortified by
Power in the stance we take.
Power is in the myth we leave when we pray.

Hope for us lives in the actions of John Brown, in
Nat Turner; in Radical Reconstruction, in the
Strength of Paul Robeson,
In the words of Claude McKay:
If we must die, let it not be like hogs
Hunted and penned
In by Jim Crow and his crows.

The people crossing Selma's bridge yell:

We will last until there are no more
Black stars falling in Alabama,
In Memphis, in America.

Every day
We survive crossings.
Every day
We meet the dawn.
Every day
We blow our horns.
Every day
We clear the air of crows' misdeeds.

We believe the promise
In a seedling, in a familial embrace,
In the clickety-clack of trains,
In braids that link colors of a diversified nation,
In the promise of feet crossing bridges,
In the promise of fresh-baked bread,
In cold lemonade.

Every day we hold the nation's note of promise,
Every day we present it for immediate cash.
Every day we wait on the bus with
Rosa Parks, who sings:

We wait for the promise of spring's flowers,
White, red, blue.

Hope is the constant companion of the determined,
Whose bare backs are rubbed raw.
Hope is in those struggling to cross quicksand.
Hope is in the house we call the White House.
Hope lives in God's house.

Remove grime from windowpanes,
Darkness can't keep morning from coming.
It's our responsibility to cross over hate,
To hear the music of the Liberty Bell,
The music of independence,
The music of freedom's siren song.

'Tis sweet you respect me.
From mountaintop to mountaintop we see
Old Glory flying from you to me.

Our country 'tis of thee
We see the rolling sea,
We see the red, white and blue
That frees me and you.

Today and every day we see
Talmadge and Faubus,
Wallace and Connor,
With crows and dogs,
Blocking the sun,
Whipping more than horses,
Hosing the likes of Buddy Boy.

Can you feel the pain?
Can you hear their claim,
Nigger, you got no right?
Our might will hold you back!

Under sun high and moon low,
Dr. King calls:

Come one, come all, come stand with me and Rosa.

This is the day we sing:

Oh Lord! We see dogs.
We feel them. Lord, we
Feel their bite.

Rosa Parks bows her head, hearing
Bull Connor saying:

Niggers, y'all come too soon.
We'll push you niggers
Off the bridge, off the ridge,
Off the ledge.
Unless Whites say so
Niggers don't have one privilege.
In the eyes of our highest court
Niggers don't have one right.

Dr. King smiles when he sees
Red, Tan, Brown, and Yellow,

Black and White
Rushing across the bridges of trouble.

The children of children
Keep coming; they keep facing
More than Bull Connor's dogs.
The people crossing, led by Dr. King, sing:

We shall overcome
We will not succumb.
We have just begun to run.

In the fury of crossing the bridge,
The strong embrace the weak,
The young, the old, the fast, the slow.

With voices full of pride,
The children of children shout:

We come from towns and cities,
From New York City, Detroit, Chicago,
From parks, fields, shacks,
From churches, schools, trails, vans,
From fields of amber waves of grain.

The inhuman behavior of crows
Shocks the world when
They bomb a church,
Killing four little Black girls.

From her seat on the bus,
Rosa Parks waves at
The children of children crossing
Selma's bridge and instructs:

Face the hoods and robes.
Face the burning crosses.
Face the hangman's noose.
Face the biting dogs.
Face the madness of Jim Crow.
Face those who ride at night.
Face the shameless who inflame.

Voices of all races, all creeds,
All religions unite calling:

Stand against
Those who defame God's children.
Let them feel His flame.
Let them face Him with their shame.
Let them hear God proclaim:
All children are my children.

Crows laugh.
They call the children of children
Crazy, because
They march, struggle, fight, die for
Qualities of life:
Liberty, Freedom, Justice, Equality.
Crazy because
They die for qualities they will never see.

Whenever they can,
Crows intimidate; they humiliate.
They make
Black people wait.
Crows call:

With God on our side, our
Power is never out of sight.
Power is being White.

Dred Scott's voice calls:

Crows cannot fasten bondages on us.
Crows believe no Black has a single right
Whites have to respect.

Crows work to keep the children of children
Stuck deep in the cloying quagmire of slavery.
Crow's business is keeping Blacks
Under White control.

Under sun high and moon low,
The children of children respond:

Rights have the power to last,
The power to correct,
The force to enforce.

Right's voice is always truer and louder,
Always purer and firmer,
Always clearer and fuller,
Than the voice that's wrong.

No opening is too small to let right in.
No door is shut too tight to keep right out.

Standing before 75,000,
In front of the Lincoln Memorial,
Marian Anderson sings:

My country 'tis of thee
Oh, sweet land of liberty
Of thee I sing.

Rosa Parks smiles her assent
When she hears Marian continue:

This is my country.
The land of the free.
What's free to you
Is free to me.

'Tis sweet, 'tis sweet
This land of liberty.
Over land and sea
We come, you and me.
We come to share equality,
What's fair for you is fair for me.

In our land of Liberty,
Oh, sweet country
Our land, our Democracy,
Our Independence,
Our Declaration,

Our flame, our flag,
Our name, America.

Together we stand under
The red, white and blue.
This bittersweet land,
Our home has room for you and me,
Room for allegory,
Room for incongruity.

Dr. King joins Marian Anderson.
Their duet,
Rising above the cheers of pride, calls:

It's up to all to perpetuate
Momentum,
It's up to all to shoulder, with decorum,
Our leader initiatives.

We know,
Americans share a single identity.
We know
Grass grows green in America.
We march, struggle, fight;
We die for qualities of life we have never seen.
We know
Grass grows green in America.
We know,
Americans share a single identity.

Fate meets Rosa Parks,

The woman riding a rising tide.

On this day, she's
Justa riding, justa sowing, justa sewing,
Justa abiding, justa calling, justa waiting.

No sir.
No sir.
Yes, that's right.

Yes sir,
I'm gonna stay . . . Right here.
I'm seated, sir!
That's right.
He can sit in the back.
There are seats.
Yes! That's correct.

Rosa Parks adjusts her red bonnet.
She smoothes her blue dress.
She folds her white hankie.
She snaps her frayed black purse closed.

Rosa loosens her shoes.
She sinks deeper into her seat.
She rests her sore feet.
Before her a red cardinal waves.

She repeats:

Yes sir!
I'm gonna stay right here.

Yes, sir!
The White man can sit
Next to the Black boy
And his mama.

She points:

There's a seat right there, sir.

Breathing deep air,
Rosa declares:

I'm gonna stay . . .
Here! Sir!

From her window Rosa Parks
Sees crows flocking,
Winging in formation.

When they arrive
Swarms of crows
Threaten, swoop, dive, and divide.

Jim Crow is frustrated.
Rosa Parks is
Parked in a front seat.
All who see her say:

She will never give up her seat;
There will be no retreat.

Rosa Parks feels the
Pull of more than gravity.
Crows crowd her.
When they begin to fall,
Rosa Parks pushes back deeper into
Her seat.

With balled fists pounding, Jim Crow screams:

The Emancipation Proclamation
Does not apply to nigras.
Nigra, you've broken our law.
Rights belonging to Whites
Do not apply to you.

You don't have one right;
Black people only have
Rights given them by Whites.
You can't sit there,
These seats are for Whites . . . ONLY.

Nigra, you have nothing to say!
Move back!
No! You can't stay in front . . . move!
Move back!

Rosa Parks settles into her seat,
She sighs and speaks:

Lord knows I'm not moving.
I'm tired.
My feet ache.
My heart is about to break.

No sir, I won't forsake
Those who've stood, and now stand,
At the same stake, justa waiting,
Justa waiting, justa waiting.

I will not budge.

No sir, No sir,
I won't move.
I'm gonna sit right here.
That's right!

I won't move, nor will I cry.
I'm gonna sit right here.
And ride, ride, ride.

The policeman says:

Lady,
You know, you're riding against the tide.

With a wry smile, Rosa nods and says:

No sir,
My patience won't expire.
No, I won't retire.
No sir,
Never, never again will I
Ride in the back.

Believe me,
I've made up my mind to
Never again sit behind,
With the sun at my back.

Never, never again will Whites
Block out the sun from me.
Never again.
No sir! No sir!
I'm not too old to understand.
Yes! I may be a mule . . . But getting up
And moving to the back
Is not what I'm gonna do!

Rosa's inner voice says:

Now is the time to realign time.
It is time to sit.

Bull Connor's dogs assail.
Rosa, Rosa is in jail.
The children of children call:

For you,
Without fail we will make bail.

The Sheriff shouts:

Enough! Enough! Enough!
Don't move! Lady, I'm cuffing you.

On the faces of Blacks
Peering from the rear of the bus,
Rosa sees years of struggle.
From those standing in the rear,
On the edge of fear,
Over the pecking crows,
Rosa hears
A mother holding a child sing:

It's me.
It's me.
It's me.
I'm moving from the back to the front.
It's time to support Rosa.
It's me.
It's me.

The conflict is not one of color.
It's not about black and white.
It's not about sitting in front or back.
It's about dignity
It's about liberty, justice, equality, democracy.

It's about freedom.
About my people's independence.

It's about my back,
It's about my feet,
It's about my mind.

It's about time.
My time.
Time to define.

Sheriff,
Sitting right here is fine.
You're wrong for standing
Between me and what's right.

Sheriff,
No one has the right to
Keep me from the sun.
The right to sit here was
Won.

Dr. King calls:
You're cuffin' Rosa Parks.

From across the nation,
The children of children chant:

Rosa won't stay in jail.
Freedom and justice will prevail.

In God's room there are
No Black seats, no White seats,
No men in hoods and sheets,
No weary road, no heavy load,
No crows that fire crosses,
No closed schools and pools,
No invalid promissory notes,
No biting dogs,
No Bull Connor, no Talmadge,
No Faubus, no Wallace.

This is the day green grass
Begins to grow in parks, in segregated
Buses, in places of learning,
Places once closed to colored people.

This is the day more than Americans
See Sister Parks sitting,
Pointing to crows in leafless trees.

Crows begin to sway before they begin to fall
And some begin to touch hands
With blacks, whites, browns, yellows, tans.

They join with those touching
Hands with Rosa Parks,
Who's planting new green grass.

The children of children call:

The qualities of freedom
Cannot be weighed, nor waived.

Sister Awareness shouts:

Grass grows green, one strand
At a time.

From fields, the children of children are
Throwing down ploughshares.
They are picking up buckets,
They are filling bags,
They are swimming, reading, readying,
They are planting grass seeds.

From Fort Wagner voices call:

There will be no defeat.
On this day victory rides.

Rosa Parks's eyes find a Black boy
Holding his mother's hand.
Overhead crows dive;
The Sheriff grins.
Rosa Parks listens to the
Young Black boy exclaiming:

Mama, I see
Green grass growing all around her.

His mother sighs and says:

There's always room in a blue sky, soon
Crows will fly away.
Son, nothing is gonna keep us
From sitting, waiting, planting grass
With Mrs. Parks.

From Selma's parks,
From Montgomery's parks,
From parks all around the country,
Voices call:

Hold on, we are with you.
We come riding buses,
We come sitting in empty front seats,
We come to clear the way
To sit with you another day.

Before crows Dr. King stands offering:

To you who oppose us,
No more lynching, lying,
No more blood and gore,
No more hanging strange fruit.

No more Fort Wagner, No more Fort Pillow,
No more lynching trees, burning crosses,
No more tarring and feathering.

No more mothers clutching babies;
Fathers falling;
Fathers fighting hoods and robes;

Families dying.
No more strange fruit dropping
On the once green grass.
No more Racial killing!

Still Jim Crow and crows murder,
Still we count the dead.
Still we wait,
Watching black, twisting ornaments
Swinging, dripping life's essence.

Through their horns, four giants,
In perfect pitch,
Dizzy and Miles,
Gabriel and Louis Armstrong, sing:

Hate injures the hater more than the hated.
Notes integrate our Star-Spangled Banner.
Notes swoop, dip, pulse, crack,
Notes sound, flirt, skip, flee, stand, beat,
Grass grows green in America.

Some notes are fast and some slow,
Some are half and some whole.
Some march and live,
Some march and die in the same breath.
All sit and all face the music.

In America the music of democracy is
Healthy grass growing on lawns of
Liberty, equality, justice.

Black notes and White notes
Share in minds, share on paper.
Side by side, in an arranged sitting,
Black and White notes participate
During the same performance.

Rosa Parks hears Dr. King tell the nation:

There is no dishonor in sitting where you are.
The magnitude of your leadership cannot be
Suppressed.

Your music makes crows restive.

With the force of oppression in his voice,
The Sheriff chides:

Dammit!
This is your last chance,
Don't let it slip away.
Move!
You don't have a damn right.
Don't hang your self, fool!

Smiling through the disgust,
Rosa Parks whispers:

Sheriff, do you hear what I hear?
My people are mowing new green grass.
The wheels of equality are in motion.
They're rolling, rolling, just rolling.

Sir,
For years I've sung your song,
Waiting for the grass to grow taller and greener.

Sir,
Try singing our song.

This is not a rehearsal.
This is the beginning.

Crows surround Rosa Parks.
They call her monkey, coon.
They call her stupid baboon.
They call her nigra, bitch, witch.

She calls:

I love green grass.
Freedom stands taller than
Men in hoods and sheets.
Freedom's call is for all to stand
On soft green grass.

Sir, the giant orator
Dr. King speaks for me
When he tells the nation:

The nature of equality is in its allocations.
It colors
All cultivated lawns
The same color, the same as

Nature enriches the sweet in
Sweet potatoes, the same as it colors
Collard greens delicious, the same as
It makes pot-liquor nectar.

Our hope is in the hammering voices
At Harper's Ferry, at Fort Wagner, at
Fort Pillow.

Our hope is the chiseled companion of
Freedom fighters, Freedom riders who
Raise the red, white and blue over
Shanties, huts, deltas, bayous.

Our hope is always growing
Like green grass waiting for the
Fullness and richness of democracy.

Under sun high and moon low
Another Black star
is rising, rising, just rising,
Rising facing the sun, facing
God's son.

Rosa Parks leans deeper into the
Ill wind to hear Dr. King preach:

Faith
Is in self, in hope, in dreams,
In the living, in facing death.

Faith
Is in the hammer and forge,
In the sun and moon,
In the land and sea.
Faith and fate
Are in the hands of Rosa Parks.

Faith is to die for what's right.
Fate melds with faith
When Rosa Parks sings,
We shall overcome.

Through the dark
Faith sits with Rosa Parks.
Her faith is divine.
Her trust is pure.
Both light the way.

Dr. King asks:

America,
How can you send our children
To fight for freedom on foreign shores
And IGNORE men in hoods and robes
Riding, from shore to shore, burning,
Destroying, murdering our people?

America,
If we share equally from the same pot,
How can white hands thrive
And black hands wither?

Every day we ask:
Why the dry wells?
Why the cracked bells?
Why the pageless books?
Why the dammed brooks?
Why the failure of Reconstruction?
Why should we ally with
Diamond Jim Brady the crook?

Why the difference
Between Black and White?

America,
Why do you support those
Who withhold our rights?
Why the anthem, My country,
The land of the free,
When you won't protect me?

Why, America,
Why the strange fruit?
Why blood on the leaves,
Why blood on the roots?

America, can't you see black ornaments
Twisting in the wind?
Every day we hear, we see
Strange fruit dropping gore
From hanging trees onto the
Greening lawns of democracy.
How long are we to bear the unbearable?

The world asks,
Why is White liberty more than
Black liberty?

Day after day, the children of children ask:

America, see more than black faces,
See us as inventors,
Creators fashioning progress:
Elijah McCoy's lubricating cup greased us into the
Industrial Revolution.
Lewis Howard Latimer's telephone patents
Revolutionized communications.
Jan Matzeliger's shoe lathe put shoes on the
Feet of the nation.
Granville T. Woods's electrical equipment
Improved the nation's railroads.

The children of children hear
Rosa Parks whisper:

The crows are crowding.
I got to sit here until I die,
Until Black and White
Butterflies, in sync, fly free
All over God's sky.

Until then I'll sit here
Until I die, until I die.

Children,
We are all the children of children.
No matter how thin
The wind we know the
Tilt of out-of-balance justice.

No matter how strong
The scent of death,
We won't move,
We'll continue to sit.

Rosa Parks screams:

Strange, strange . . .
Strange fruit . . . drops.

Over Memphis the shot, the
Scream floods the nation:

Again she screams:

Nothing will ever be the same.
Our Black star . . .
Our brother is dead . . .

Somebody assassinated
Our giant brother.

He delivered his last message
In a country long on waving:
The Red, the White, the Blue;

But short on protecting his
Dissenting voice.

His last song rings:

From the mountaintop I have
Seen the river.
Death is my shadow.
God's light shows me the way to glory.
Today and every day I ask . . .

Why in this country won't lush grass grow
Beneath the feet of Blacks?

Why does this country praise God yet
Provide allowances for the murdering Klan?

Today under sun high and moon low,
Crows celebrate the death of the
Fallen Black star

Standing on the mountain, Dr. King shouts:

I know the sun and the moon.
I know God's call.
He calls in the spring,
In the winter, in the summer,
In the fall.
I know the way home.
I know when he calls
I will fly and not cry.

This I know,
God's sun will always shine, shine, shine.
This I know,
God is calling, God is calling.

Under sun high and moon low,
Rev. King, Sr.,
Hears the muffled roll of death:

Rap, Rap, Rap, Rap, Rap,
Rap, Rap, Rap, Rap, Rap,
Rap, Rap, Rap, Rap, Bang.

Hear me, America.
I am, I am
The son and the father
Of a Black man.

King,
Martin Luther King, Sr., is my name.
With the blaze of God's glory in my eyes,
I raised, and now again I raise,
God's child, Martin Luther King, Jr.,
To the sky.

God, let not this child,
Our son,
Die in vain.

Wherever he is, protect him;
He's on his way.

Keep him at your side, Lord.
Crows crucified him.

Lord, another Black Star rising
Over green grass, rising over
Stone Mountain, rising over
Democracy, another star in the
Red, White and Blue.

America, hear this son of a Black man
Proclaim:
The climate will change; his
Ripples will grow into waves.

Americans shout:

Our son, a Black Star, is buried beneath
The greening grass of Democracy.

On the horizon trees sway,
Birds flock, white roses bend still.
Children dressed in white
Form a circle.
Roses release the color of blood.

Tellit, tall and innocent,
Hair in a fresh cornrow,
From the village of
Shout It Out, Tennessee,
Hesitates before she

Steps forward to sing over
Dr. Martin Luther King, Jr.'s
Open grave:

America,
This land of sweet liberty
Is your land, my land, our land.
My country 'tis of thee
Includes you and me.

He touched me and you,
One people, one nation,
One commitment, one purpose,
One soul, one country, one flag,
One sun, one will, one spirit,
One greening lawn of democracy.

This is your opportunity
To open wider the doors of
Liberty and equality.

Still we wait. Still we wait
For you to correct a deliberate wrong.
One love under God's roof.
God's love needs no proof;
The Black Star has fallen.

One voice, one hand, one heart,
One God, one son, one life,
One moon, one sun, one day,

One lawn of green,
One sunless day, one sky,
One love, one in God's spirit.

Over one open grave,
In the land of the brave,
In the land of liberty and democracy,
One Black star shines no more.
We celebrate the life of a king.

His hands reached into the sky.
He anointed the children of children,
Who kneel, who march, who parade.
He takes all to the mountaintop.
He preaches humility lives in humanity.

This day
A hush, a hush
Falls.

On the grave
Falling
Red roses
Break the hush.

Tellit whispers:

Hush now, hush now,
God's redeeming sun
Shines on his fallen Black son.

The King's soul shines.
Never,
Never will we forget you.
Never will we wonder about
The pitter-patter of soothing rain.
There's enough grain for grass.

During the hush of morning,
Dew crowds America's lawns.

Hush now!
Just the clickety clacking of
Democracy's train.
Going around, above, and below the ground.

Hush now!
Just the sound of dirt
Filling our brother's grave.
Hush now!
Just the muffled drumbeat,
Just parading feet, hush spills.

Just why? Just why?
Just anguish, just a sigh,
Just the horse's whinny.

Just the crack of the caisson wheels
Crushing green grass,
Just solitary grieving voices,
Just a mother speaking:

There's enough love to go around.
Hush, hush.
There's no need to cry.

Hush now,
Hold his flame high.
Forge your world.

Hammer the impossible into possible,
Hammer hate into understanding,
Hammer brown grass green.

Dr. King stood his ground,
Showing us how to survive,
Touching us for life.

Under sun high and moon low,
The children of children call:

Unearth treasures, retrieve drums,
Smooth brows, straighten the crook
In elbows.

Tellit, the willowy girl from
Shout It Out, moves over the dirt
Covering the fallen star's
Grave. She spreads grass
Seeds over the mound.
When the seeds flutter in the wind,
She sings:

What a bitter taste of water.
Crows stand in fields of spotted yellow corn.
Today, yesterday's sweet water is bitter.

What's the meaning of
Seeds blowing free in the breeze,
Over the green grass of Democracy?

What's the meaning of
Brittle grass shimmering
Under December's midnight sun?

Today, Tellit's tart tongue calls:

Sweet, sweet was yesterday.
Today human frailties ride the
Darkness of winter.

The nation is blue.
A king is buried in the ground.
Down by the riverside, the nation cries:

We have a right to sing the
Blues.

Dirt, just dirt, just trampled grass,
Just grass worn through.
No seedlings peeking
Through the bloody earth.

Only the
Birth of screaming Blues,
Only
Raw eyes, only ears listening,
Only
Quivering lips praying.

Only mud baking in the sun,
Only the song of bleaching
Bones.

Only waiting, just waiting for
Jim Crow's wrongs to end, only
Waiting for his song of hate to grow thin.

Only the nation's silence,
Only caring hands filling cracks,
Only a broken heart,
Only survivors waiting
For brown grass to turn
A soft welcoming green.

Only grieving,
Only voices calling,
Dyin'. Only cryin'.

Only waiting for yesterday's and today's
Fumbling to turn another
Worn page.

Only rustling memories,
Only falling leaves,
Only waiting to break bread
Together on our knees.

Let us knead the threads of America
Into a democratic mosaic.
Let the music of those on the margin
Of the rich green lawns sing:

God bless America.

America, hear me:
I am a child of faith,
I live in the center of green grass.
I long for something to call home,
A place where the pitter-patter of
Rain soothes, a place where the
Clickety clacking of Freedom's train
Rolls, just rolls
Over the green grass of spring.

From the nation's capital,
Congressional voices join Tellit in song:

'Tis sweet, 'tis sweet, our land of Liberty.
'Tis sweet, our country
Owned by you, you, and me.

Tellit calls all:

Be you Black or White,
Yellow, Red, Brown, Tan,
We are brothers and sisters,
Speak up.

No more, no more, no more
Strange fruit blowing in the wind.
No more blood on leaves,
No more blood in roots.

Together we stand ringing
Freedom's bells that praise the
Spiritual gift of humanity.

Great is the human cup.
Those who drink from it cannot
Quench thirst for love of family.

Rap-rap-rap-rap-tap
Tap-rap-rap-tap-tap
Rap-tap-rap-tap-rap
Independence calls:

Turn over America's fertile
Soil, plant trees, spread seeds.
Carefully tend the green lawns until
Justice, liberty, equality
Shine brilliant on our flag, until

The stars on the field of blue
Embrace the Declaration,

All humans, in the eyes of the creator,
Are His Children.
Children, standing before Dr. King's grave, sing:

Where do stars go when the sun shines?
What does the wind say to the leaves?
Why do bees' wings flutter?
Why do strong trees bend?
Why does grass grow greener, taller,
Fuller in a Democracy?
Why must a Democracy
Include every variety of grass?
Why must all streams and rivers flow
Free to the sea in a Democracy?

America, heal.
We sit on the same green grass,
Sowing the colors of red, white and blue.
America, from this moment on, we drink
From the same bottomless well of Democracy.
We sit in a moment of history.
This is our country.

From the cemetery,
The children of children see
Rosa Parks shaping
A dramatic moment in history.
She sings:

We will not stand on
The ashes of the dead.

Standing on green grass,
Rosa Parks states:

Every flower must have a clear view
Of the green lawns facing the river.
Every flower is
Independent of every other flower.
Flowers are in perfect harmony with nature.
Every flower is rooted deep in Democracy.

Harmony is
One nation, one people, one well,
One balanced scale of
Liberty, opportunity, equality,
No aristocracy,
Just you and me sharing
Equally the riches of our Democracy.

On America's lawns there is
No need to discuss authenticity,
No need to discuss citizenship.
Our claim leaves no room for doubt.

All around the country,
Two distinguished giants,
Paul Robeson and Malcolm X, call out:

Rosa Parks hears
Feet running, wheels rolling,
Blackbirds, magpies, doves, blue jays,
Arriving to drink from deepening wells.

From a bandshell in Selma, Alabama,
They hear Kate Smith singing:

God bless America the beautiful,
The land where birds fly free,
Where sweet well water is ours.

Paul, Rosa, and Malcolm,
Shapers of the moment, declare:

Together we put down ploughshares.
Together we nurture America's greening grass.
Together we turn half-truths into whole truths.
Together we oppose the Ku Klux Klan.

Under a spacious sky,
Birds of all kinds are
Gliding free from shore to shore,
Over purple mountains,
Savoring the harvest of the fruited plains.

This is the day Rosa Parks
Eyes the Midnight Special and smiles, saying:

Every day freedom fighters,
Laborers, ditch diggers, hog carriers, pickers,
Builders: ship builders, bridge and
Tunnel builders, carpenters,
Teachers, preachers, florists, mothers,
Fathers, brothers, sisters,

Steeple climbers, ladder climbers, mountain climbers,
Welders, iron workers, roofers, painters, paraders,
Flute players, piano players, drummers,
Arrangers, composers, recliners, pullers,
Persuaders, beggars, drivers, divers,
Dissenters, entertainers, bookkeepers,
Dealers, singers, signers of
The Declaration of Independence
Go into the night.

Old and young, Black and White
Americans are singing:

No more, no more, no more
Turning back, no more moving back.
No more swallowing salty tears.

God sheds his grace on purple mountains,
On the face of this land of Liberty.
He sheds his grace on
You and me.

God sheds his grace on the foolish and wise,
The big and small, the weak and strong,
The simplest, the thoughtfulest.

God sheds his grace on the gawkers,
The hookers, the candlelighters.
God sheds his grace on the cake makers,
The caretakers, the candle makers,

The tinsmiths, blacksmiths,
The families called Smith, Jones,
The family called Mr. and Mrs. America.

Rosa Parks sitting with freedom
On her mind, hears a familiar echo:

Move, nigger.
I've done shot a bunch of coons.

A familiar echo reverberates:

No, no,
No, not husband,
Not father, brother, not son, not lover.
No, Sheriff, not John,
Don't kill another.

The epitaph:

Here lies a dead nigger
Shot because he wouldn't move
From a front seat to the back.

Rosa Parks pushes deeper into her seat,
Her bosom heaving,
Keeping her appointment with destiny.
She wails:

I'm sitting on more than hope.
I remember
Everyone who died . . . sitting in this seat.

The long night begins.
More riders join
Her quest than yesterday.
She recites:

Nothing will separate us again,
Not race, not religion, not creed,
Not origin of birth.

We come from the same seed.
That which creates you, creates me.
The love that nurtures you, nurtures me.
The hands that rock you, rock me.
The voice that soothes you, soothes me.
The arms that cradle, cradle both of us.

I sit bloodied, unbowed by threats,
Wearing garments worn by ancestors,
Washed in the tears of ancestors.
On this day I hold fast,
Preparing for a long fight.

I know the connection between
Wind and message,
Fire and passion,
Foundation and structure,
Wonder and birth,

Largesse and mirth,
Allegory, legend, myth.

From jagged mountains, from deltas,
From riversides, from farmers harvesting,
From North, South, East, West, from hamlets,
From cities big and small,
Americans shout:

Let no sad song of discrimination be sung
On the lawns of Democracy.
Let us satisfy this
Historic moment with nobility.
National responsibility cannot wait.

History's moment allows only one take.
Humanity, humility, solemnity connect
Our commitment to freedom and liberty.
This is the time to correct inequality.

Through the winds of change the
Stars and Stripes demand
One people, one flag, one anthem,
One Star-Spangled Banner.

Rosa Parks sees her
Grandmother and Grandfather smoothing
Their coveralls, clearing years of caked
Mud from their shoes.
Rosa laughs and smiles when
They call to her:

You are God's gift
To the children of children.
Hold fast, grandchild;
We know you are unmovable;
We are with you.

Rosa Parks stiffens her resolve, humming:

Through threats, through yelling,
Through clubbing, through biting dogs,
Through men dressed in hoods and robes,
Through lynching, burning, killing,
Through man's inhumanity,
I sit, waiting.

My sun will not go down,
Not even when crows boast:
We done kilt another nigga,
Move, nigra;
Soon your feet won't touch the ground,
You'll be dead . . .

These words will
Be the last sound y'all
Ever hear, nigra.

Whispers from ancestors' burial grounds
Seep, filling the moment:

Sweet, sweet is the moment.
Sweet is Rosa's black rising star.

Sit child, sit like the rock of ages.
Truth won't ever let a lie hide in peace;
There's no hiding place in a cloudless sky.
Sit child! Just sit!

Every day the children of children recite:

We love a clear sky, fertile soil,
Space, a place to plant seeds,
We love full citizenship.
End Jim Crow. End Segregation.

Rosa Parks prays:

Precious Lord,
Take my hand.
I rise with these words every day:

Democracy, Justice, Liberty, Opportunity,
Equality, Freedom, Country, America,
Citizen, Human rights, You,
Me, Individual, Flag, Red, White, Blue,
United, One, Nation, Inalienable rights,
Pursuit of happiness, Promise, Honor,
Trust, Truth, Honesty, Home,
Family, Faith, Fate, Sun, Moon,
Life, Death, Belief, God.

Lord, we all breathe the same air.
Nobody owns the soil of Democracy.

Democracy is shared by one people,
One country, one America.

December 1, 1955,
Jim Crow's barrier is shattered;
382 days after the Mongomery boycott,
The United States Supreme Court's decision reverberates:

Montgomery, Alabama's
Segregation on public transportation
Is illegal.

Ancestors whisper:

A child leads,
Rosa Parks's
Action transforms.
The last red leaf clings.
There's room for new leaves.

Another lilac blooms,
The nation calls:

There are many variations of green.
Healthy grass is not biased.

America is still the land of spacious skies.
America is still the land of purple meadows.
America is still the country where it's all right
To strive, to ride, to seek, to fine and refine.

On healthy lawns,
There's room to be pensive,
To lessen the anger of raging crows.
On healthy lawns,
There's room for our song to echo:

We shall overcome.
We stand with Tiny Shiny, Running Boy,
Evalina, Banjo Pete, with Americans
Who share the same belief,
America is the land of the free,
The land of liberty, unity.

Our salvation is in the music of the Delta,
Of New Orleans, of New York City,
Of Chicago, of Kansas City.

Those joined with Rosa Parks sing:

In our new music,
We express our anguish,
Strengthen our resolve, fortify our spirit.
The music of our salvation supports our
Internal wealth, wealth in hope, wealth in faith.

The source of America's wealth is in music
That causes the heart to race, leaves to swing,
Black and white notes to integrate
When they navigate the score.

Afro-American music,
The collective music of our soul,
The orchestral soul of our indomitable faith,
Is heard in the downbeat, the upbeat,
The beat that repeats.
We create our music: Spirituals,
Gospel, Hymns, Blues, Jazz
To liberate our spirit,
To share with humanity.

From her seat Rosa Parks softly calls:

Share buttered beans,
Collard greens, cornbread;
Share language, books,
Knowledge, thoughts.

The longer I sit on the margin of democracy,
The louder the Blues singers' song drapes the day
With longing, waiting, pining.
The tighter we hold, the harder crows peck.

Every day Blacks cling to
The constant message of God.
Every day Blacks ask:
What realm of love is it that
Denies our rights?

And every day the children of children are
Wiser, smarter, tougher, stronger.

Every day they advance, opening
New paths to new highways, waterways,
Towns, cities, new opportunities.

In the moment when chaos is shattered,
Old Glory flies higher and higher
Over Rosa Parks's head.
No matter what happens to her
She will not move to give a White her seat.

The voice of America's conscience sings:

We admire the will of Rosa Parks.
We admire
Her stamina to sit through grief and terror,
Her ability to keep night from devouring her strength,
Her ability to keep doubt,
Laced with crippling apprehension,
From reaching her soul.

The children of children call:

Rosa Parks winds a new clock every day.
Historic deeds are never far away.
For Rosa Parks the kaleidoscopic moments
Covering her seem slow.

Every day, while waiting for bigoted
Mores, rules, and Jim Crow to crumble,
Her resolve to avoid mistakes grows, knowing

A life lost cannot have a retake.
History's moment allows only one take.

When she stands and smoothes
Her hair with her hand
The children of children hear:

Till the Jordan rolls no more,
I am gonna just sit . . . Here.
Lord, I hear you say
Don't move, don't explain.

Just fill bags with more and more seeds,
Just sow row after row, don't complain,
Just sow, just sew patches, don't explain,
Just fill, just fill, just fill more than bags,
Fill schools, colleges, universities, just
Fill pools, don't complain, don't explain.

Lord, I'm praying to you for
Just an unobstructed view, just a view of
Grass growing in America, just a view of a
Spacious sky, just the majesty of
Lady Liberty holding
High the torch of freedom.

Lord, death stands ready;
It rides with us.
We pledge to die before
We give up our seats.

We are ready to face
You, our loving God,
Crown us all with good.

Don't explain, don't complain.
America, just see the purple mountains,
Just enjoy waves of amber,
Just share the grains,
All Americans are the same.

The prayerful voice of Calli declares:

One lady's word, No! was the beginning
Of many words that merge,
Converge, convey, sway,
That show the will to go beyond the river.

December 1, 1955, lives.
Blacks hum a hymn:

Rosa, sit where you are,
Truth sits with you.
Sacred is your soulful song.
Go ahead and call them . . .
The police.

Jailed and fingerprinted
I am a prisoner of racial injustice.

Rosa Parks hears
The wind carrying
The voice of the dead:

Honor our bleached bones.
Don't scatter our ashes.
Don't move from your seat.
This is the moment to sit in the seat
Of your choice.
Sit where you are.
Breathe deeper, freer.

Rosa Parks prays:

God always makes room
This is the day we fill our bags fuller
This is the day on buses
We sit without restrictions.

On this day the force of our song
Resounds.
We Shall Overcome

Today, December 1, 1955,
We move to solid high ground.

Saturday, November 10, 2001,
Mississippi's Governor Ronnie Musgrove
Declares it Freedom Riders Day
Mississippians, stand with me
Righting wrongs Jim Crow committed,

Beating, burning, tarring, maiming,
Murdering Blacks struggling to end segregation
On public transportation.

In Alabama, Rosa Parks replies:
No sir, I won't move back.

Throughout the nation crows threaten:

Nigger, you better git
Your Black ass out of that seat.

Rosa Parks sings:

My seat is the rock of ages,
I won't move.

Every day we ask
Why does the cracked bell
Swing stiffly before people of color?
Why the difference in Black and White
Justice and equality?
America, what's the meaning of
The Stars and Stripes forever?

The light of national shame is on
The frail Black lady sitting between
Right and wrong;
She's setting the table.

Still she waits.
Deep in the valley where crows nest,
The children of children sing:

Got my own mind; White folks don't
Know me.

Still, fields of cotton and sugarcane are picked.
Still sowing seeds, still caring for seedlings,
Still harvesting more than fruit, still burying
The murdered. Still counting new immigrants
On the green lawns moving ahead of us;
Acquiring more fruit; more power,
Still setting other people's tables.

Still waiting for full citizenship,
Still pledging allegiance to
The United States of America.
Still singing "My Country 'Tis of Thee"
Still saluting the red, white and blue,
Still committed to the land of liberty.

Still unblocking streams,
Still running, carrying,
Calling, singing, climbing,
Still refusing to move.
Still spilling angst,
Still crows' contempt
Hinders our advancement.

Still a nation of inequality
Still the nation prays for God;
To shed his grace on America.

Still great is unequal justice,
Still man' laws conflict with God' laws,
Still moving to higher, firmer ground,
Still singing the Blues.

Lord,
Still, at the end of the tunnel
Intense light shines,
Still our soul is open to the sunny side
Of life's river.

Lord,
Still we create music
That makes feet tap, fingers snap,
Hands clap, hips sway.
Still the music of today draws
People closer to notions
Of
Oneness.
Oneness that
Responds
To
Sound,
To
Touch,
To
Smell,

To
Taste,
To our soul.

Still on this day, July 24, 2001, we are waiting for the
Grass, on the margin, beneath our feet, to grow
As plush, as soft, as tall, as inviting, as attractive,
As pliable, as compelling and complete, as it is
In the center of the great lawns of Democracy.

Still our eyes flash, flush with anticipation.
Still we honor
America
In Song,
In Dance,
In Prayer.

Rosa Parks recites:

In Gospel, in rhythm,
In Folk music, in Spirituals,
Our Soulful music swings,
Helping Black people to
Groove, to survive the
Burdens of Monday to Friday, to
Praise and surrender our soul on Saturday, to
Celebrate God on Sunday.

Our song is the collective music of our spirit.
Our song resonates with black birds.

Still, rhyme and rhythm
Coalesce with lyrics and melody.
Still, black and white notes meld
Rich harmony with soulful spirituality.

Rosa Parks hears
The children of children's song:

Still gotta hold on for one more minute,
One more step,
One more Supreme Court decision.

Still step by little step, we move
Closer to the river,
Closer to lawns.

The voices of presidents Kennedy and Johnson
Sang to the country:

Still, Blacks on buses
Are being forced to move
From the front to the back,
Forced out of pools and schools.
Still, Rosa Parks's
Questions go unanswered:
Will injustice ever end?
Can democracy thrive?

The children of children call:

We will not be turned around.
Still we wait.
Still we wait.
Still we will not
Move to the backseat.

Still humans are the
Highest living form
Of God's creation.

Still we rejoice knowing the
Humming bee sings
Its sweet song of freedom.
Still we seek unity,
Still we will not be denied.

Still we wait.
Still, with civil rights
And affirmative action,
Our suffering continues.
Still a lower living standard,
Still the question is asked
Is this the day?

Rosa Parks calls:

We have families,
We build homes,
We serve God.

Singing the Star-Spangled Banner,
We celebrate our citizenship
When we mix pigments
Of red, white and blue.

With humility we pay homage to those
Who made the sacrifice of life over safety
To insure our freedom.

The nation must guarantee
We will not be pushed
Over a steep ledge.
Still the bias stains.

Still we are mothers and fathers,
Sisters, brothers, and sons,
Loved ones and lovers.
Still we are one.
Still falling ashes of
Restless martyrs dress the moment.

Still cawing crows scream:

We's kilt more than a few niggers.

Still the stench of tar burning on flesh,
Still the smell of buckshot
Boring into shattered bone,
Still our fire burns beneath desire.

Still sweating,
Still trying to please the majority,
While preserving
The rap-tap-rap-rap-tap
Of integrity;

Still the clickety clack, clack of the train,
Still its wheels sing the songs of incomplete freedom.
Still sorrow spills,
Still crows murder more than a few.

Still the plaintive songs of our odyssey are sung.
Still loving life, still yearning,
Still hearts beating, still waiting,
Still needing, kneading, believing.

Still seconds pass into minutes, into hours.
Still another generation waits.
Still another season.

Still disappointment has no cushion.
Still hoping, exalting,
Still liberty's bells are tolling.
Still the cadence of our journey
Is found in the grass
That holds our footprint.

Still trying to fill the space between a
Whisper and a murmur that asks:

Why must we wait?
Why do grapes bruise?
When will we sit with giants
At the great table?

Calli calls:

All God's children are equal.
Still imperfect are man's deeds.
Still Rosa Parks's feet hurt. Still she
Sits and still Black people wait.
Still America is our home, and
Still sophistry is heard.
Still the orchestra within us plays.

Still cawing crows yell:
Surely you remember,
Goodman, Schwerner, Chaney?

When we get a hold of you
Y'all won't be so bold.
Y'all will know what it means to be cold.
Niggers, y'all won't ever be ready.

Still we wait and still we ask:

What form of American
Justice denies us our human rights?
Surely denial doesn't come from above?
And yet every day is a maiden day,

And every day waiting
Knits generation after generation.

Rosa calls:

Don't make an allowance;
Not even an ounce!

The children of children exclaim:

Still after decades of waiting
We hear the same language,
Wait,
Be patient, your time will come.
The wheels of justice and equality are slow.

Still Rosa Parks waits, singing:

Fact,
Shining stars give light.
Daylight breaks, twilight falls, night covers,
Rain and snow spill
Beneath the drooping tree.

Fact,
Swollen rivers flood, a blooming cherry tree
Fills with fruit,
A pollinating bee flutters,
A hummingbird hums, honey is a treat.

Fact,
I will sit in the first empty seat.

Fact,
A moment shapes history.

Fact,
I will not move to give a White
Person my seat.

Fact,
I'm doing what's right.

Fact,
The angry tyranny of the authority
Handcuffs, fingerprints,
Jail, bail,
The fine—fourteen dollars.

Judicial force misused
To reinforce a wrong.

Fact,
Still Blacks sit
Waiting for right to correct wrong.

Fact,
Martin King, Jr., is livid,
His voice booms:
The boycott of buses ignites;
Embers of unity begin to spark,

Spreading the seeds of our
Deepening determination.

Fact,
World focus is on Montgomery,
Alabama, where empty bus seats spill.

Fact,
Blacks are thrilled when
International voices shout,
The boycott is effective.
We see out-of-control crows,
In the country of green lawns,
Bullying a frail, middle-aged woman.
It's America's national disgrace.

Freedom riders
Join Rosa Parks chanting:

Oceans roar, seas
Wash debris from sure to shore.
God,
I hear Mary
Weeping, her son
Hangs
Between two thieves.

God All mighty, where's the dignity?
We wait, knowing someday
The murdering will end.

Day after day,
Devils dressed in hoods and robes
Kill more than thin grass.

Still the earth rotates around the sun,
Still the stars, moon, and planets are
One with the universe.

Linked arm in arm,
Calli of the valley and Rosa sing:

Lord, the sky is slow to open to our cry.
Still the seasons come and go.
Still spring's rainbow's colors glow.
Still rivers flow, still perching eagles search
Waiting for prey.

Still expectations . . . stumble for . . .
Complete citizenship with all of
Democracy's fruit stumbles.

Still the boycott grows.
Still humble, still patient we wait.

Still Black people pray,
Knowing soon on America's green lawns,
They will equally partake in
Democracy's full plate.
Still knowing our
God will not forsake
Us.

part three

Celebration of Survival

Mounted Guerrila
(war Independence 1895-1898)

Rosendo M. Cintrón   Luis M. Rivera   Pedro A. Campos—   Felisa Rincón de Gautier

Gathering giants facing the
River stand to speak:

God, with your help
We turn dark to light,
We turn angst into soulful songs of
Our people.
We fight the Black Code,
We fight the fugitive laws,
We fight crippling mores.

No! no, no, the world hears our nos.
The world hears the children of children call:
This is the land of the free,
The country of equality.

We Americans work to correct
Democracy's incongruity,
Its inequality, its injustice.
We Americans must
Bridge the differences between
Race, religion, creed.

On the lawn of democracy
Rosa Parks sits,
Fending off flocking crows, praying:

Please stop the carnage, God.
Please send us
Harmony, inclusion, peaceful uniformity.

Under sun high and moon low,
The children of children call:

On our way to the river we bond,
We bridge, we develop opportunities.
Down by the riverside, we cultivate togetherness;
Orchards replete with
Red apples, golden peaches,
Brown pears, black grapes.

Lord,
Just beyond the river,
Down by the riverside,
Before the celebration,
We set the great table for
Our giants and their children,
Who tell us,
Words, deeds, and faith have
Weight,
Who tell us,
Our might comes from years and
Years of waiting, believing,
Knowing, and honoring.

Standing before the table all sing:

Hallelujah, hallelujah
We believe in
The Father, the Son,
The Holy Ghost.

Under a forgiving Son,
Roses are crimson,
The red leaf hangs,
Lawns grow greener; togetherness
Richer, fuller.

The full fruit of Democracy is
Still out of reach for us
We are told
To be patient.

Still the nation's promise clings,
Still the effort to convince us
Cloying unfertile dirt is
Equal to caressing grass.

With heads bowed celebrants call:

Still, after generations,
We carry, we push, we pull.

We follow directions
To the lawns facing
The River which is
Just over the hill,
Just around the bend,
Just beyond the creek.

Just wait.
Soon you'll enjoy
The sweetest fruit.

Soon you'll sail
Unencumbered on the River.

Calli of the valley
Warns while waiting:

Don't ever step
On ancestors' burial grounds.
Always remove shadows
Covering their tombstones.
Watch out for crows.

Hope deepens your faith,
It lessens despair.

The children of children yell:

What a waste, what a waste.
Our days are spent listening to
Promises, speeches, sermons,
Attending meetings that
Try to persuade us to wait
A little longer,
To move a little slower.

Again, we are told,
Before demanding a full share
Of democracy's fruit . . .
Equal rights, equal treatment,
It's better for the country
To move . . . slower.

After years of waiting,
The children of children respond:

We are experts in experiencing
The illusion of sincerity,
The growing weight of crumbling
Insincerity,
The resentment of ineffective
Commitment.

Across the lawns of Democracy, their voices sing:

In the wake of repeated disappointments
We shoulder the added weight of
New laws, additional amendments.

With hope, we step from decaying grass
To the narrowing seams of racial separation.
Where we wait for aggressive enforcement
Of existing laws, directives, policies, initiatives.
Still with guarded belief,
We wait for fuller implementation.

Still waiting, we recite:

Fish swim, birds fly, preachers preach,
Blues singers shout,
The time is . . . right now!

Musicians arrange, compose,
Create, perform music
Written on once white sheets;
The time is right now!

No! No! No!
No more will
We bite our cheek.
No more will
We hold our tongue.

We know
Our opposition to existing policies
Births diversity, nurtures solidarity,
Challenges incongruity, supports liberty, repels
Infidelity, supports unity, bridges and bonds
Our songs of humanity and equality.

We know
We are the sons and daughters of
One God.

The children of children call:

Every day from Sunup to Sundown our
Moments are spent thirsting,
Waiting for court decisions,
Overcoming derision, our moments
Are spent revising, reversing opinions,
Criticisms.

Still we wait while
The tables of
The Declaration of Independence,
The Constitution,
The Bill of Rights,
Human Decency
Are set.

From Harpers Ferry to
The Civil War, to Fort Wagner,
To Reconstruction,
To the Freedman's Bank,
To the promissory note
Of forty acres and a mule,
Still we wait.

From presidents presiding over
World Wars, One and Two,
The Korean conflict, Vietnam,
To senators, to Congresspeople,
From judges and juries,
To pioneers, to preachers, to professors,
To laborers, to caregivers, to providers,
To the well-intended, to arms that gather,
To hips that call, that hold, that welcome
The seed; hips that cherish the precious gift,
Life. We still stand watching,
Listening, praying, waiting.

Day after day, at Democracy's gates
We patiently wait,

Demonstrating our unshakable faith.
The children of children recite:

Good Lord,
We yearn for the country where
Liberty, justice, freedom live
Free from Jim Crow's tyranny.

We feel
The full weight of disenfranchisement, the
Weight of disjointed insincerity,
The weight of empty broken promises.

After decades of waiting,
After decades of holding
The weightless note of
Hollow promises,
We know the struggle
It takes to sweeten
Bitterness.

We know
The absolute weight of unfair;
We know
The absolute cost in lives
To correct what's unfair.

Standing with the children of children
Calli of the valley sings:

Harriet Tubman – Frederick Douglass – Ida B. Wells – Monroe Trotter – Dr. Wm. B. Du Bois – AnnaMarcus Garvey – Dr.Martin L.King

Soul singers, spiritual singers, jazz and gospel
Singers, Dixieland and folk singers, choir and
Chorale singers, and blues singers
Gather in towns, in villages, in
Hamlets, in deltas, by riversides.

Over pounding drums,
Over lilting flutes,
Over souls praying,
Over the joy of fish frying,
Over wafting apple pie,
Under the Stars and Stripes,
Giants, legends, spirits
Of all races
Gather at the great table to celebrate
The songs born in the
Soul of Black Americans,
Songs that speak to dignity lost
To slavery.

After a deep sigh,
That spans the loss
Of freedom to slavery,
Rosa Parks's song resonates clearer:

Today pine needles and cones fall as one.
Today under the sun,
Moral certainty births power.
Today
The children of children are playing

Kick the can, pick-up sticks,
Hopping, skipping, jumping.

Today I hear
Strumming guitars, blowing bugles,
Children bouncing with joy,
Tweeting, chirping birds,
Squealing lemurs climbing higher, faster,
Bellowing lions roaring louder.

Today
When the Statue of Liberty turns and
Points its bright torch in our direction and
When her arms open wider
I know the great table is set.

The Supreme Court
Of the United States declares:

On this day, May 17, 1954,
Separate educational facilities
Are inherently unequal.

Still, after years of waiting,
Rosa Parks calls:

Black and White Americans are inextricably
Linked, linked like green is to grass,
Like red, white and blue are to America,
Linked like liberty, justice, and equality
Are to the Bell of Liberty,

Linked like the baking cake
Is to the oven,
Like promise is to honor.

Rosa Parks declares:

I'll sit here till I die,
I'll sit here till I die,
I'll sit here till
The wafting peach pie
On the windowsill
Fills the sky.

I'll sit till the mournful trumpet
No longer sings taps,
The cross no longer burns,
Sheets, hoods, and robes no
Longer hide crows,
Until there are no miscues, no missteps.

I'll sit here until the children of children
Sing,
There are enough peaches
In the world to share with everyone.

Rosa Parks smoothes her graying hair, calling:

I'll sit here till the winds of tolerance
Caress level grass.
I'll sit right here until
The children of children remove the

Boundaries separating Blacks
From equality.

I'll sit until crows' shadows stop covering
Greening lawns,
Until their shadows no longer hang
Lower and lower,
Obscuring banners
Carrying my message; the children's
Message!

From where I sit, I see
Oak trees' arms opening full,
Allowing majestic lights to dress
Purple mountains with
Amber fields of grain.

I hear the children of children
Widening paths,
For the giants,
Buddy Boy, Black Tiny Shiny,
Tubman, Truth, Ma Rainey, Garvey,
Booker T., DuBois, Dr. King, Paul Robeson,
John Brown, Adam Clayton Powell, Jr.,
Turner, Malcolm X., a man,
Son rising, just rising—
America's flag higher and higher

I see the children of children striving
To keep our nation from favoring

One race, one creed, one religion,
One political party over another.

After rubbing her hands together
Rosa Parks calls:

Lord, I know faith opens gates.
I pledge,
At our table there's always
Room for another.
No citizen will ever be turned
Away from democracy's lawns.

When the sun brightens her face
She stands reciting:

It's up to all Americans
To set a balanced table.

The children of children call:

With checks and balances,
It's up to all to
Keep the lawns of
Democracy
In an intense light.

Surveying the gathering families,
From the knoll overlooking
The great table,
Rosa Parks informs:

In the name of one humanity,
In the name of one family,
The great table is set.
All are linked, celebrating,
Yes, celebrating
Life, liberty, love,
National unity.

America
We keep sowing seeds,
We keep coming,
We keep forging larger bells,
We keep digging deeper wells,
We keep filling our bags,
We keep boarding trains,
We keep creating every day.

With a rock in hand,
Grandmother leans to Grandfather
She whispers:

David defeated Goliath with this.

When Grandfather throws
The rock at cawing crows,
Crows scatter, dive, and die.
She claps, then asks:

Do you see what I see?
The table is set

Overhead, cawing crows are busy
Devouring the day's sown seeds.

Around the great table,
I see Calli of the valley, linking her
Arms with the children of children
Who link their arms
With the giants and their families:

Black Tiny Shiny, Buddy Boy, Evalina,
Maudell Sleet, Banjo Pete, See See Rider
And his daughters, Insight, Understanding, and
Awareness, who are embracing Phillis Wheatley,
Mary McLeod Bethune, and Shirley Chisholm, who are
Hugging Frederick Douglass, who's acknowledging
The spirit of President Abraham Lincoln, the spirit of
Martyrs, Goodman, Emmett Till, the Scottsboro Boys.

Harriet Tubman's arm is linked in
Sojourner Truth's arm;
A red, white and blue shawl covers
Truth's heaving chest.

John Brown and his family
Of twenty freedom fighters are
Linked to Nat Turner.

Smiling giants quickly make room for
Colonel Robert Gould Shaw and his
Family, the heroic freedom fighters,
Men of the Massachusetts 54th.

Lordy Lordy Miss Claudy stops
Singing the Blues when
DuBois, Garvey, Dr. King, Jr.,
Malcolm X, and Booker T. Washington
Link arms with
Robert Johnson, Samuel Johnson, Howlin' Wolf, Lead Belly,
Bessie Smith, Billie Holiday, Mahalia Jackson,
Marian Anderson, Paul Robeson, Dinah Washington,
Ruth Brown, Big Mabelle.

Sitting in the middle of the great table,
Joe Louis and Sugar Ray Robinson
Link arms with
Jackie Robinson, Satchel Paige, Jesse Owens,
Wilt Chamberlain, Michael Jordan, Jim Brown,
Big Daddy Lipscomb.

God's messengers, Dr. King,
Daddy Grace, Father Divine,
Adam Clayton Powell, Jr.'s arms
Are linked to
Writers and their families:

Toni Morrison, Pilate and Sula,
Rita Dove, Thomas and Beulah,
Alice Walker and The Color Purple,
Sterling A. Brown's "Strong Men,"
Ralph Ellison's Invisible Man,
Richard Wright's Native Son,
James Baldwin's The Fire Next Time,
Gwendolyn Brooks's "We Real Cool,"

Langston Hughes's "The Negro Speaks of Rivers,"
And "Song for a Dark Girl,"
Paul Laurence Dunbar's "Worn Out,"
James Weldon Johnson's "Lift Every Voice and Sing,"
Yusef Komunyakaa's Neon Vernacular,
Margaret Walker's "For My People,"
Ida B. Wells's A Red Record,
Zora Neale Hurston's Mules and Men,
Jean Toomer's Cane,
Claude McKay's "If We Must Die."

At the head of the table,
Swinging in a jam session,
Miles Davis, Louis Armstrong, Milt Hinton,
Ben Webster, Ella Fitzgerald, Sarah Vaughan,
Dinah Washington, Charlie Parker,
John Coltrane, Lester Young,
Gabriel, Orpheus, Duke Ellington, Count Basie.
They call out:
God, please look down,
God, won't you look down.

We see, we see
Nothing can stop us now,
Nothing can keep us
From the river.
We see no more waiting.

Lord, crows scatter when
Our music rocks.
They can't carry another lie,

Not another lie.
When crows attempt to rise and fly
They hesitate and flutter, then
They dive like rocks, falling rocks,
Falling from the sky,
Death arrives.

Joyous voices led by Martin Luther King, Jr.
Around the table joyous
Voices sing:

Since
The beginning of our existence
We loved light,
We loved butterflies,
We loved the sun, moon,
We loved the sky full of
Twinkling stars.

We loved bumblebees,
Flowers and trees.
We loved the fullness of grass
Beneath you and me.

Every day,
While on our knees
We fire the gift of our spirit.
We create a soulful melody.

Every day,
We rise knowing

Nothing can stop us,
Nothing can stop us from
Coloring the fire that burns within.

Rosa Parks sings
With the children of children:

No haze can daze us,
No lie can bind us,
Nothing can keep us
From the earth, from the sky, from
Water, wind, and fire,
From humanity's desire to be free.

Nothing can keep us
From the family of man
That binds you and me to unity.
We are one to eternity.

Holding Grandfather's arm,
Grandmother leans to him, whispering:

Do you hear the children of children calling:

We are not refugees;
We are on firmer ground.
Nothing can stop us . . .
NOW!

glossary

ABOLITIONISTS—EARLY FREEDOM FIGHTERS

James Armistead (December 10, 1748–August 9, 1830) James Armistead was a Colonial spy during the American Revolution who posed as a slave and fed false information to the British army. Having worked the British side, Armistead returned to the Colonial forces, passing inconspicuously through British lines, and conveyed to Lafayette what he had observed about British troops and their movements and plans. His knowledge was instrumental in the capture of General Cornwallis and the British surrender at Yorktown, Virginia, in 1781. Armistead had to appeal for his freedom, but it was granted, and he lived out his days as a free man and a farmer. He is remembered as an American patriot, a freedom fighter, and one of the original Black soldiers.

John Brown (May 9, 1800–December 2, 1859) Born in Connecticut into a family violently opposed to slavery, Brown initially became involved in militant activity to prevent Kansas from becoming a slave state. The government offered Kansas the right to determine for itself whether it would become a slave state or a free state, and resolve the issue on its own. This was equivalent to making the state into a battleground between those who opposed slavery everywhere, and those who felt entitled to own humans in bondage anywhere they pleased.

Brown is best known for his raid on Harper's Ferry, where he fought his final battle and was martyred for the cause of liberating Black slaves. Brown and his men intended to seize the weapons stored at Harper's Ferry, and with those weapons arm southern slaves so that they could fight for their freedom. This plan was derailed by various fighting men under the command of Robert E. Lee. Two of Brown's own sons lost their lives as the small group at Harper's Ferry fought to the end and were unwilling to surrender. Brown was so uncompromising that as his own son lay dying in agony and begged to be shot, Brown encouraged him to "die like a man," which he did shortly afterward. The aging Brown, his personal dreams shattered—as DuBois would have us picture—was captured and hanged in a trial presided over by Lee. John Wilkes Booth was present at the hanging.

John Brown's raid escalated events leading to the Civil War. Southern states became alarmed that northerners and abolitionists would advocate further military activities such as Brown's, and began to defend their position accordingly by capturing Fort Sumter. This Southern military occupation provoked by Brown was unacceptable to President Lincoln and his belief in the preservation of the Union.

"John Brown's Body Lies A-Mouldering in the Grave" sung to the tune of the "Battle Hymn of the Republic" became an inspirational song for Union troops as they marched into battle against the South.

Cinque (c. 1813–c. 1879)   Born Sengbe Pieh in West Africa, Cinque was kidnapped by slave traders and thrown on board a Portuguese ship bound for the Caribbean. Cinque pried a nail loose from the ship boards between decks, where the slaves were packed like cargo, and with that humble weapon forged a rebellion. Many slave ships were the scene of uprisings, with the slaves fighting against abduction and inhumane treatment, but on the *Amistad* the struggle turned out in favor of the Africans. The crew was subdued and many of them killed. The surviving sailors were ordered to turn back to West Africa, but the navigators duped their former captives and sailed up the coast of America instead. Off the coast of Long Island the *Amistad* was captured by the U.S. Coast Guard, and Cinque and the rest of the West Africans were taken to Connecticut, where their troubles were only beginning. Between 1839 to early 1841, their case moved from the circuit court to district court, and then to the Supreme Court where they were acquitted, and for the third and at last final time. The court's decision on the *Amistad* went against the requests of Spain, which insisted on ownership of the boat and its human cargo, pressuring President Martin van Buren to prolong the case and appear before the Supreme Court. The Supreme Court also upheld the rulings of the lower courts and rewarded the West Africans freedom and safe passage to their native land. Chief Justice Taney, a southerner who infamously presided over the Dred Scott decision, and who also swore Abraham Lincoln into office, was a member of the Supreme Court during Cinque's trial. When Cinque returned to his village, he learned that his wife and children had been abducted during his years of absence.

Frederick Douglass (February 14, 1818–February 20, 1895)   Born as Frederick Augustus Washington Bailey, into slavery in Talbot County, Maryland, he became known as Frederick Douglass. He was also called "The Sage of Anacostia" and "The Lion of Anacostia." Douglass learned how to read and write in secret while he was still a slave, a forbidden privilege. Because of his antipathy to his condition, Douglass received many whippings. Once to avoid being whipped he fought and defeated a slave breaker, Edward Covey, in a two-hour fight.

Douglass escaped and wrote several famous abolitionist narratives, among them, *My Bondage and My Freedom* and *Narrative of the Life of Frederick Douglass*. A renowned and charismatic public speaker and newspaper editor, Douglass spoke and wrote on Black education, the condition of the Black race, and women's rights. Douglass worked tirelessly to convince Abraham Lincoln to allow Black soldiers to fight with the Union army in the Civil War. In 1872, Douglass was nominated as the vice presidential candidate on the Equal Rights Party ticket with Victoria Woodhull, the first woman to run for president of the United States.

Harper's Ferry   The sight of a U.S. Army arsenal that John Brown attempted to capture in "John Brown's Raid." Located in Jefferson County, West Virginia, at the confluence of the Potomac and Shenandoah where Maryland, Virginia, and West Virginia meet.

Dred Scott (1799–September 17, 1858)   A humble man, Dred Scott found himself entangled in a controversial Supreme Court case and its aftermath far beyond anything he might have dreamt of when he innocently appealed to the courts for his freedom. Scott had accompanied his owner to and lived for a time in Illinois, a "free" state, which according to the law at that time entitled him to his freedom. However, the Supreme Court upheld the opinion that enslaved Blacks were property and had no rights no matter where they traveled, into a "free" state or otherwise. This verdict confirmed the rights of Southern slave owners to pursue their valuable property—their slaves—even into the free territories, in order to get them back. However, the decision deepened discord with Northern abolitionists, and freedom fighters like John Brown, which inched the divided country toward the Civil War. Obscured by the war, Dred Scott did gain his eventual independence from slavery, and he and his wife lived out their lives and died free people in St. Louis, Missouri.

Sojourner Truth (c. 1797–November 26, 1883) Sojourner Truth was born into slavery. Originally named Isabella Baumfree, she was born in New Paltz, New York, where slavery existed until 1827. Isabella endured a fate similar to slaves in the South—separated from her mother and father in a slave auction, punished by the whip, and subjected to many severe hardships—so she escaped in 1826.

By 1843, she took the name Sojourner Truth, and like the definition of her name, she became a traveling preacher. She would go on to become a popular speaker on issues such as the abolitionist movement, women's suffrage, and getting jobs for former slaves once the Emancipation Proclamation was signed into law. She also advocated for a "Negro State" in the west, for a period of time.

Harriet Tubman (c. 1820–March 10, 1913) Born Harriet Ross into slavery in Maryland. She lived an extraordinary and exemplary life; tough and uncompromising, she was a woman of legendary experience, strength, and wisdom. When she was a child, she was hit in the head by a lead weight thrown by a master at another slave. Suffering from a fractured skull, she was indifferently returned to her plantation where she lay for two days, unattended and disregarded. Once she was well enough to walk, the young child was sent back out into the fields, the blood still flowing from her wound and mixing with her sweat as she worked. From that time on she was plagued by headaches and sleeping spells, but she acquired an acute spirituality, and an uncanny acumen and understanding. On many occasions she intuited that something of importance was about to happen, or avoided capture in her daring escapades.

Her first escape was with her brothers who feared for their lives, had second thoughts, and several weeks from the plantation they all returned. Undaunted, Harriet escaped on her own. Securing her own freedom wasn't enough, so she returned to liberate her family, and then returned from the North again and again as a fearless "conductor" on the Underground Railroad. She liberated so many slaves that she was reverently named "Moses" by the enslaved and abolitionists who knew her.

Nat Turner (October 2, 1800–November 11, 1831) Nat was an intelligent and deeply religious individual who believed he had been called upon by an angry God to fight back against the hostile abuse of slave owners. In 1831, Nat organized a rebellion, and revealed to slaves and slave owners alike that Blacks would not remain passive to humiliation, violence, and mistreatment indefinitely. Turner's rebellion caused the death of fifty-seven White men, women, and children. The rebellion was suppressed within forty-eight hours, but Nat managed to escape and hid in a hole in a field for several weeks until he was discovered by a curious dog that innocently sniffed out food Nat had stored in his hiding place. On November 5, Nat was tried, convicted, sentenced to death, and then hanged on November 11 in Jerusalem, Virginia. His body was mutilated by an angry mob seeking revenge. Nat's death and the violation of his corpse turned him into a martyr to slaves and abolitionists alike.

CIVIL RIGHTS MOVEMENT

James Chaney (May 30, 1943–June 21, 1964) In 1964, James Cheney, Michael "Mickey" Schwerner, and Andrew Goodman, as members of CORE (Congress Of Racial Equality) were helping the Freedom Summer Project by assisting in registering Black voters. On the morning of June 21, 1964, the three men set out for Philadelphia, Neshoba County, to investigate the recent burning of Mount Zion Methodist Church by the Ku Klux Klan because it was going to be used as a Freedom School. After visiting the church, on their way back to the CORE offices in Meridian, Mississippi, the three men were arrested. They were later released and told to leave the county. As they headed out of town several Ku Klux Klan members stopped them on a secluded road, shot them dead, and buried their bodies in an earthen dam.

With the help of an FBI informant, the bodies were found two months later and nineteen men were arrested for the murder. Only seven of those men were found guilty of conspiring to deprive Goodman, Schwerner, and Chaney of their civil rights.

Civil Rights A movement in the United States aimed at allowing African Americans to vote, while abolishing segregation and racial discrimination.

Theophilus Eugene "Bull" Connor (July 11, 1897–March 10, 1973) Bull was a police official in Birmingham, Alabama, during the American Civil Rights Movement. He was a member of the Ku Klux Klan, and a staunch advocate of racial segregation. As the Public Safety Commissioner of Birmingham, Alabama, in the 1960s, Connor became a symbol of bigotry. He infamously fought against integration by using fire hoses and police attack dogs against protest marchers.

Andrew Goodman (November 23, 1943–June 21, 1964) One of three civil rights activist who were murdered by the Ku Klux Klan during Freedom Summer in 1964. *See James Chaney.*

Martin Luther King, Jr. (January 15, 1929–April 4, 1968) The son of Alberta Williams King and an Atlanta preacher, Reverend Martin Luther King, Sr. In 1954, at the age of twenty-five, King became pastor of the Dexter Avenue Baptist Church in Montgomery, Alabama, and in 1955 he received his doctorate in philosophy from Boston University. While a student, King studied Mahatma Gandhi's nonviolent methods of civil disobedience. In 1959, King visited Gandhi in India, and the trip inspired King to a life of nonviolent resistance and a commitment to African Americans' struggle for civil rights. While at Boston University, King also met his wife, Coretta Scott, with whom he had four children and who accompanied and supported King during his fight for equality.

In 1955, King gained national prominence when as a twenty-six-year-old minister he organized the Montgomery, Alabama, bus boycott. The boycott was a show of Black support for Rosa Parks, who refused to give up her seat on a segregated Montgomery bus, shortly after the murder of Emmett Till, and the boycott opposed segregation on the public transit system.

King's leadership initiated the modern civil rights movement. King led many nonviolent marches that were significant moments in the history of civil rights. Among them was the march on Washington for jobs and freedom in August, 1963, during which he delivered the famous "I have a dream" speech at the Lincoln Memorial, as well as the Selma to Montgomery marches in 1965 for African American voting rights in the South. One of the Selma marches was called "Bloody Sunday" because lawmen attacked the peaceful demonstrators with billy clubs, tear gas, and bull whips.

Following his work for equal rights in the South, King began to organize protests for economic justice, the unfairly imposed hardships of life in Northern ghettos, and opposition to the Vietnam War.

King was an inspired public speaker and his speeches are textbook examples of rhetorical mastery. In 1964, at the age of thirty-five, King became the youngest person to receive the Nobel Peace Prize for his efforts to end segregation and racial discrimination through civil disobedience and other acts of nonviolence. He donated the prize money to the civil rights movement. On April 4, 1964, in Memphis, Tennessee, King was assassinated by James Earl Ray. Although he had spoken on many occasions about the possibility of a violent end, only the day before he had delivered his moving speech, "I've been to the mountaintop," expressing his acceptance of death in the service of a greater cause. In 1986, his birthday became a national holiday, making him the first non-president to have a holiday in his honor.

Martin Luther King, Sr. (December 19, 1899–November 11, 1984) Led Ebenezer Baptist Church in Atlanta, Georgia, married Alberta Williams King, father to: Martin Luther King, Jr., Albert Daniel King, Willie Christine. An active civil rights worker.

Malcolm X (May 19, 1925–February 21, 1965) Born Malcolm Little in Omaha, Nebraska, Malcolm's father was most likely killed by White supremacists for his civil rights work and his mother was committed to an institution a few years later.

Malcolm, a sharp student, was discouraged from achievement so he dropped out of the predominately White school he attended. Later he became involved in petty crimes and was eventually arrested for burglary, which carried a ten-year sentence. It was in prison that he was introduced to the teachings of Elijah Muhammad and the Nation of Islam (NOI).

As a member of the NOI, Malcolm strictly adhered to the teachings of Muhammad, which included remaining celibate until his marriage to Betty Shabazz in 1958. Malcolm came to be deeply hurt by the deception of Muhammad, whom he had considered a living prophet, when asked to cover up Muhammad's affairs and subsequent children. Malcolm also felt guilty about the masses he had led to join the NOI, which he now felt was a fraudulent organization built on too many lies to ignore. The lies and his belief that the civil rights message he was advocating went beyond Muslims would lead Malcolm to leave the NOI. He would go on to found the Muslim Mosque, Inc., and the Organization of Afro-American Unity in 1964.

That same year, Malcolm went on a pilgrimage to Mecca, Saudi Arabia. The trip proved life altering. For the first time, Malcolm shared his thoughts and beliefs with different cultures, and found the response to be overwhelmingly positive. When he returned, Malcolm said he had met "blond-haired, blue-eyed men I could call my brothers." He returned to the United States with a new outlook on integration and a new hope for the future and when he spoke, instead of just preaching to African-Americans, he had a message for all races. Less than a year later, he was assassinated in Washington Heights on the first day of National Brotherhood Week.

James Meredith (June 25, 1933–) Born in Kosciusko, Mississippi, of Native American (Choctaw) and African American heritage, Meredith enlisted in the United States Air Force right out of high school and served from 1951 to 1960. He then attended Jackson State College for two years and applied to the University of Mississippi, but was denied admittance twice.

On October 1, 1962, he finally became the first Black student at the University of Mississippi. His enrollment, virulently opposed by segregationist governor Ross Barnett, sparked riots on the Oxford campus. Federal troops and U.S. Marshals were sent to the campus by President John F. Kennedy. The riots led to a violent clash, which left two people dead, including French journalist Paul Guihard. Forty-eight soldiers and thirty U.S. Marshals were injured with gun wounds. Barnett was fined $10,000 and sentenced to jail for contempt, but he never paid the fine or served time. The charges were dismissed by the Fifth Circuit Court of Appeals. Bob Dylan sang about the incident in his song "Oxford Town."

Meredith's enrollment is regarded as a pivotal moment in the history of civil rights in the United States. He graduated from the University of Mississippi on August 18, 1963, with a degree in political science.

Ronnie Musgrove (July 29, 1956–) This Democrat was the sixty-second governor of Mississippi from 1996 to 2000. Musgrove was recognized nationally as a leader among his peers, serving as chair of the National Conference of Lieutenant Governors and as vice chair of the National Governor's Association.

In 2003, Musgrove sent a letter praising Judge Roy Moore's display of the Ten Commandments in his courthouse, calling it "the basis for our legal tradition." Musgrove announced that he would call on other governors to display the monument in their state capitols as well. In 2001, Musgrove signed legislation requiring the motto "In God We Trust" to be displayed in every public school classroom, as well as school auditoriums and cafeterias, throughout the state.

During Governor Musgrove's tenure he made a controversial decision to keep the Mississippi state flag, which featured the Confederate Battle Flag. The flag was a cause for great contention between Blacks and Whites. The Confederate flag is seen by many as a symbol of racism and bigotry, often used by White supremacist groups such as the KKK.

Rosa Parks (February 4, 1913–October 24, 2005) On December 1, 1955, Rosa Parks was arrested for refusing to give up her seat to a White passenger on a city bus in Montgomery, Alabama. Parks's actions inspired over 42,000 Blacks to participate in the Montgomery bus boycott in order to desegregate the city's buses. The boycott lead to the U.S. Supreme Court ruling that public bus segregation is unconstitutional and put Parks, Martin Luther King, Jr., and the civil rights struggle into the national spotlight.

Adam Clayton Powell, Jr. (November 29, 1908–April 4, 1972) Known as "Mr. Civil Rights," Adam Clayton Powell, Jr., was the preeminent civil rights leader in the United States from the 1930s through the '50s. Powell was born in New Haven, Connecticut. His father, Adam Clayton Powell, Sr., was a Baptist minister and headed the Abyssinian Baptist Church in Harlem, New York.

Powell had a confrontational and unconventional disposition that many found troublesome. He attended City College of New York, but flunked out to the displeasure of his father, who encouraged Powell, Jr., to return to college. Powell attended Colgate University in upstate New York, and then he enrolled in Union Theological Seminary, and Columbia University Teachers' College, where he received a master's degree in religious education. Thus the pastorate of the Abyssinian Church was passed from father to son.

Powell, Jr., became a leader in Harlem and

in the New York Black community. He organized rent strikes, picket lines, and fought for civil rights, equal pay, clothes, food, and affordable housing. He was elected to the city council of New York in 1941, and was elected to the U.S. Congress in 1945. He was charismatic, had a reputation for flamboyance, and a tumultuous political career, but voters from Harlem loved him unconditionally and elected Powell, Jr., year after year until June 1970 when he was defeated in the Democratic primary by Charles B. Rangel, who has represented the area ever since.

In 1960, Powell took over as chairman of the House Education and Labor Committee, where he made his greatest contributions. He oversaw passage of President Kennedy's "New Frontier" and President Johnson's "Great Society" social programs, in addition to an anti-poverty bill, an increased minimum wage, and the National Defense Education Act. At one point Powell was expelled by members of the House, so he took the case all the way to the Supreme Court and won back his seat.

Michael Schwerner (November 6, 1939–June 21, 1964)   One of three civil rights activist who were murdered by the Ku Klux Klan during Freedom Summer in 1964. *See James Chaney.*

Scottsboro Boys   On March 25, 1931, nine Black teenagers (Haywood Patterson, Roy Wright, Clarence Norris, Andy Wright, Willie Roberson, Charles Weems, Ozie Powell, Olen Montgomery, and Eugene Williams), ranging in age from thirteen to twenty-one, got into a fight with several White teenagers on a train. As the Black teenagers were being arrested for fighting, two White women, Victoria Price and Ruby Bates (who would later recant her story and become a witness for the teens), falsely accused the group of rape.

The Black teenagers were tried several times, repeatedly found guilty, and sentenced to death

by all-White Southern juries, before they were eventually set free. The injustice of the case garnered international attention and sympathy for the Black youths and civil rights in America.

Emmett Till (July 25, 1941–August 28, 1955)   The civil rights movement of the 1950s and '60s began with Emmett's death. Emmett Till was a fourteen-year-old African American from Chicago who was infamously murdered during a visit to his uncle in Money, Mississippi. Emmett violated Jim Crow etiquette and spoke "inappropriately" to a White woman in a grocery store. A few days later several White men came and took Emmett from his uncle's home in the middle of the night. He was beaten and shot before his body was dumped into the Tallahatchie River.

Two of the abductors were later identified and put on trial. They were acquitted after less than thirty minutes of deliberation. The injustice of the trial was seen worldwide and was a motivating force behind the civil rights movement of the 1950s and '60s.

Ida B. Wells (July 16, 1862–March 25, 1931)   Wells was a fearless anti-lynching crusader, suffrage and women's rights advocate, journalist, and passionate fighter against racism. Born the child of slaves during the Civil War, Wells lost her parents and baby brother to a yellow fever epidemic. She and her remaining siblings lived with various aunts and uncles after her parents' death. Wells went to work as a teacher in Black schools and continued her education by attending Rust College in Memphis, Tennessee.

In 1884, she refused to give up her seat to a white man on the Chesapeake & Ohio Railroad line and travel in the Jim Crow car, preceding Rosa Parks by seventy-one years. When the conductor tried to throw her out of the car, she "fastened her teeth on the back of his hand." Eventually the conductor with the aide of two men dragged her out. Ida returned to Memphis, hired an attorney, and sued the railroad. She won her case in the local circuit courts, but the railroad company appealed to the Supreme Court of Tennessee, which reversed the ruling. This was the first of Wells's battles for civil rights to which she tirelessly dedicated the rest of her life.

After the incident on the Chesapeake & Ohio line, she entered the world of journalism when she received offers to tell her account of the incident on the train, and about her suit against the train company. Soon after she began telling her story, she was fired from her teaching job and became a full-time journalist.

In 1892, three of her friends were lynched. Horrified, Wells began to write about lynching in her newspaper, and encouraged the Black residents of Memphis to leave the city. A mob in turn ransacked and destroyed the offices of her newspaper. She was advised not to return to Memphis under peril to her life. In 1909, she went on to help found the National Association for the Advancement of Colored People (NAACP).

Walter Frances White (July 1, 1893–March 21, 1955)   In 1918, he joined the small national staff of the NAACP in New York at the invitation of James Weldon Johnson. White acted as Johnson's assistant national secretary. In 1931, he succeeded him at the helm of the NAACP, a position he held until his death.

Under his leadership, the NAACP set up the Legal Defense Fund, which raised numerous legal challenges to segregation and disenfranchisement, and achieved many successes. Among these was the Supreme Court ruling in *Brown v. Board of Education,* which determined that segregated education was inherently unequal. He was the virtual author of President Truman's presidential order desegregating the armed forces after the Second World War. Under White's leadership, the NAACP's membership quadrupled to nearly 500,000.

Roy Wilkins (August 30, 1901–September 8, 1981)   A prominent civil rights activist in the United States from the 1930s to the '70s, Wilkins was an active member of the National Association for the Advancement of Colored People (NAACP), and between 1931 and 1934 was assistant secretary under Walter Francis White. When W. E. B. DuBois left the organization in 1934, Wilkins replaced him as editor of *Crisis,* the official magazine of the NAACP. In 1951, Wilkins was named executive secretary (the title was later changed to executive director in 1964) of the NAACP.

In 1950, Wilkins along with A. Philip Randolph, founder of the Brotherhood of Sleeping Car Porters, and Arnold Aronson, a leader of the National Jewish Community Relations Advisory Council, founded the Leadership Conference on Civil Rights (LCCR). LCCR became the premier civil rights coalition, and has coordinated the national legislative campaign on behalf of every major civil rights law since 1957.

CIVIL WAR

Black Soldiers   Black soldiers had great difficulties to overcome in order to enlist in the Union army during the Civil War and join the battle to end slavery. At the outset of the war, Abraham Lincoln was slow to consider the question of allowing Blacks to fight as even in the North the issue was too politically and socially divisive. There was prejudice toward Blacks and Lincoln was forced to act with restraint. In time, and in the necessity of war, Lincoln's restraint eroded and the Emancipation Proclamation of January 1, 1863, cleared the way for Black soldiers to join the war effort. In battle, Black soldiers faced extreme perils. Confederate President Jefferson Davis had issued a proclamation of his own declaring that if captured in battle, Black soldiers would be returned to their former states and to slavery. As a result, Black soldiers not only faced the possibility of death on the battlefield, but also the possibility of being murdered if they were taken prisoner or forced to surrender—similar to the incident at Fort Pillow (*see Fort Pillow*). Over the course of the war, Black soldiers earned the recognition of their fellow soldiers, and distinguished themselves by many acts of bravery and courage.

The Civil War (April 12, 1861–April 9, 1865) The American Civil War was caused by political disagreements between the North and South states. The South felt they were being unfairly taxed. They also had issues with growth of the Republican and the Northern states' political power and felt the government, especially in regards to slavery, was not considering their needs.

When Abraham Lincoln won the election without winning one Southern electoral vote, the South states began passing ordinances of secession and formed their own pro-slavery government under the leadership of Jefferson Davis called the Confederate States of America.

The war began when Confederate forces attacked a U.S. military installation in South Carolina in 1961. The war would continue for the next four years and over 600,000 Americans would die. In the end, the North would win, slavery would be abolished, and a stronger government would be created.

The 54th Massachusetts Infantry The 54th Massachusetts Infantry was one of the first official Black units in the United States armed forces and in the Civil War. Commanded by Colonel Robert Gould Shaw, initially the 54th was not permitted to fight, and only performed manual labor. However, the soldiers of the 54th slowly earned respect. They became famous for their assault on Fort Wagner, South Carolina, on July 18, 1863. The 54th lead the assault on the fort, which was heavily defended and fortified. Shaw died in the

battle, and the Black soldiers were driven back in fierce hand-to-hand combat as they scaled the walls of the fort.

Nathan Bedford Forrest (July 13, 1821–October 29, 1877) On April 12, 1864, Confederate general Nathan Bedford Forrest led his thousand-strong Confederate troops against the Union-held fortification at Fort Pillow in Henning, Tennessee; defended by 570 soldiers—half White and half Black. After surrendering, unarmed Union soldiers were pursued and massacred. Nathan Forrest was the first Grand Wizard of the Ku Klux Klan.

Fort Pillow On April 12, 1864, Confederate general Nathan Bedford Forrest led his thousand-strong Confederate troops against the Union-held fortification Fort Pillow, Tennessee, which was defended by 570 soldiers—half White and half Black. After being overwhelmed in the battle and fearing the threat of being captured by Confederate troops and being a large contingent of Black soldiers, confusion and panic overcame the defending Union soldiers, who began to scatter fearing for their lives. They were pursued by the Confederates and shot down in what became regarded as a "massacre." For the duration of the war, the battle cry for Black soldiers was "Remember Fort Pillow!"

Fort Wagner Fort Wagner measured only a few hundred yards in both length and width and was located on a small island in South Carolina. The fort protected the approach to Charleston harbor, and was heavily fortified, very difficult to approach only along a narrow spit of beach. The Confederate soldiers were deeply entrenched. Despite days of bombardment, when the Union infantry began their assault there was fierce opposition and they suffered heavy casualities. At dusk on July 18, 1863, the 54th, led by Colonel Robert

Gould Shaw, at last fought their way into the fort, but were driven out in hand-to-hand combat and Shaw was killed. However, the battle of Fort Wagner revealed the bravery of the Black soldiers of the 54th, and that they would fight as well as any White regiment.

Gettysburg Address (November 19, 1863) A speech delivered by President Abraham Lincoln at a dedication ceremony four months after the Battle of Gettysburg. The Battle of Gettysburg took a brutal toll on the lives of men on both side of the war. In this speech, President Lincoln explained why we were at war and that we were fighting for "a new nation, conceived in Liberty, and dedicated to the proposition that all men are created equal."

The Gilmore Medal Named after General Gilmore, commander of the battle at Fort Wagner, the Gilmore Medal was awarded to the survivors of the 54th who fought in that battle.

July 18, 1863 On July 18, 1863, Robert Gould Shaw and the Black soldiers of the 54th assaulted Fort Wagner, South Carolina. Shaw was killed in the battle, but the Black soldiers of the 54th, one of the first all-Black Union regiments, displayed tremendous courage and bravery and have been long glorified for their heroism.

Robert E. Lee (January 19, 1807–October 12, 1870) On the Confederate side, Lee is one of the most beloved and famous generals in the American Civil War. He graduated second in his class from West Point and served with distinction in the Mexican-American War.

When the Civil War started Lee was offered a position with the Union army, but chose to resign his commission and join the Confederate Army. Lee joined the Confederacy and advised President Davis and the Secretary of Defense. In 1862,

Lee was commanding the Army of Northern Virginia and becoming known for his strategic ability. Under his command the army won several battles against the Union. In 1863, he was defeated at the Battle of Gettysburg and surrendered to General Ulysses S. Grant, effectively ending the war.

Colonel Robert Gould Shaw (October 10, 1837–July 18, 1863) Shaw accepted the opportunity to lead the 54th Massachusetts, the first all-Black Union regiment, in the fight with the Confederate army during the Civil War. Prejudices about Blacks, stereotypes that they could not fight, that they would make poor soldiers, that they were lazy, existed everywhere in early American society. However, Shaw was willing to stake his reputation on this abolitionist undertaking, while many other officers found the command objectionable, or beneath the dignity of a White Union officer. As Shaw came to know and respect the men in his regiment, he developed sympathy for their cause. Shaw joined his men in a protest for equal pay and adequate clothing for his soldiers, and helped earn their trust and respect. But his affection for his Black soldiers is best remembered when he selflessly gave his life leading the charge on Fort Wagner in South Carolina.

EDUCATORS

Mary McLeod Bethune (July 10, 1875–May 18, 1955) An educator and civil rights leader, Bethune is best known for starting a school for Black students in Daytona Beach, Florida, that eventually became Bethune-Cookman University.

Born in South Carolina to parents who had been slaves, Bethune took an early interest in her own education. With the help of benefactors, Bethune attended college hoping to become a missionary in Africa. When that did not materialize, she started a school for six Black female students.

The school later merged with an institute for Black boys and eventually became the Bethune-Cookman School. Its quality far surpassed the standards of education for Black students, and rivaled those of White schools. Bethune worked tirelessly to ensure funding for the school, and used it as a showcase for tourists and donors, to exhibit what educated Black people could do. She was president of the college from 1923 to 1942 and 1946 to 1947, one of the few women in the world who served as a college president at that time.

Bethune worked under presidents Calvin Coolidge, Herbert Hoover, and Theodore Roosevelt on child welfare, housing, employment, and education. In June of 1936, she was assigned director of the Division of Negro Affairs, and became the first Black woman to serve as head of a federal agency. As director, she traveled across the country, speaking out for equal education and treatment for Blacks.

Shirley Chisolm (November 30, 1924–January 1, 2005)   This congresswoman from New York City—the first African-American woman elected to Congress—became the first African American from a major party to run for president of the United States. She received 152 first-ballot votes at the 1972 Democratic Nation Convention.

Prudence Crandall (September 3, 1803–1890)   Established Canterbury, the first Black female academy.

In 1831, Prudence Crandall, educator, emancipator, and human rights advocate, established a school, which became the first Black female academy in New England at Canterbury, Connecticut. The establishment of this school later resulted in her arrest and imprisonment for violating the "Black Law." Although she was later released on a technicality, the school was forced to close after being harassed and attacked by a mob.

W. E. B. DuBois (February 23, 1868–August 27, 1963)   Born William Edward Burghardt DuBois in Great Barrington, Massachusetts, he was one of the most influential Black leaders of the first half of the twentieth century. DuBois shared in the founding of the National Association for the Advancement of Colored People (NAACP) in 1909. He served as its director of research and editor of its magazine, *Crisis*, until 1934. DuBois was the first African American to receive a Ph.D. from Harvard University, which he attended on a $250 scholarship. He graduated cum laude. Through his research and studies, DuBois concluded that in a climate of virulent racism, social change could only be accomplished by agitation and protest.

At the turn of the century, DuBois had been a supporter of Black capitalism. By 1905, he had been drawn to socialist ideas and remained sympathetic to Marxism throughout his life. DuBois acted in support of integration and equal rights for everyone regardless of race, but his thinking often exhibited a degree of Black separatist-nationalist tendencies. In 1961, DuBois became completely disillusioned with the United States. He moved to Ghana, joined the Communist Party, and a year later renounced his American citizenship, becoming a citizen of Ghana. On the eve of the March on Washington, DuBois died in Accra, Ghana.

Marcus Mosiah Garvey (August 17, 1887–June 10, 1940)   By the age of fourteen, Garvey, who dropped out of school to become a printer apprentice, led a strike for higher wages. From 1910 to 1912, Garvey traveled through South and Central America and the United Kingdom. Inspired by what he saw around the world and by the works and writings of Booker T. Washington, who impressed Garvey with his philosophy of self-improvement for people of African descent, Garvey came back to Jamaica and formed the Jamaica Improvement Association, which evolved into the United Negro Improvement Association (UNIA) in 1914.

Two years later, Garvey moved to Harlem, New York—known as the negro capital of the world—where he established the headquarters for the UNIA. As Garvey's ideas expanded, he became a Black nationalist.

Garvey founded *Negro World*, a popular weekly newspaper that conveyed his message of Black pride, and he launched several other African-American capitalist ventures. In 1920, he presided over an international convention of Black people in New York, where he called for freedom from White domination in Africa.

Garvey experienced a character assassination in 1923 when he was convicted of mail fraud when selling stock in his failed Black Star steamship line. This business was to be the beginning of international trade among Black nations and Black peoples. Garvey was sentenced to five years in prison. As a result, many of his other ventures failed as well, including an attempt to foster Black colonization to Liberia—part of his "Back to Africa" movement. After his release from prison in 1927, Garvey was deported to Jamaica. In 1934, he moved to London, but he never regained prominence.

Booker T. Washington (April 5, 1856–November 14, 1915) Born a slave, Washington went from working salt mines in West Virginia to working his way through school after being emancipated, first at what would become Hampton University, then at Wayland Seminary. Washington went on to found Tuskegee University in Alabama, which he presided over until his death.

Washington believed Blacks should work their way toward acceptance through hard labor and self-reliance—not necessarily through protesting. He was criticized by the leaders of the NAACP, especially W. E. B. DuBois, who demanded a harder line on civil rights. After being labeled "The Great Accommodator" by DuBois, Washington replied that confrontation would lead to disaster for the outnumbered Blacks, and that cooperation with supportive Whites was the only way to overcome pervasive racism in the long run.

Although he did some aggressive civil rights work secretively, such as funding court cases, he seemed to truly believe in skillful accommodation to many of the social realities of the age of segregation.

FICTIONAL CHARACTERS

Angela Sixteen-year-old sister of Buddy Boy. A dancer.

Baby Infant; beginning notion.

Banjo Pete Banjo Pete, Evalina's husband, Maudell Sleet's grandson, is a gifted banjo player. He is a strong field hand but prefers playing his instrument. Banjo Pete plays on street corners, in back rooms, at dances, and mostly at small social gatherings or just sitting and staying meaningfully occupied. While Banjo Pete plays he laughs with the delight of a child at the chords that are invented out of the banjo, so he generally laughs as he plays. The banjo is a treasured instrument from Africa and holds many memories.

Black Tiny Shiny From a broken home, Black Tiny Shiny is generally inconspicuous and overlooked. Black Tiny Shiny has a great intellectual ability admired by those who know him best, but he is a modest teenager and unostentatious. His people know he is unique and look up to him, but his invisible nature gives him the name "Tiny." The mysterious glow that radiates within him makes him "Shiny." Masters and crows use his name derisively, but suffer a misinterpretation of Black Tiny Shiny believing that no light can emanate from his "blackness." Black Tiny Shiny disregards people, has two minds for those who disrespect him or treat him diminutively. He laughs, eats well, and grows strong. Black is the light that can never be snuffed by war, plagues, abduction, or slavery. Black Tiny Shiny carries the light that is given to him by his God.

Brothers Intelligence, Intellect, Wisdom related to See See Rider, Mother Awareness, Sista Awareness, Sista Understanding, Sista Insight, and Sista Angela.

Buddy Boy No known family, from a broken family that was separated from their family and sold into slavery. Older brother of Angela and Nexus. At twenty years old, he's one of many running to catch Freedom's train . . .

Calli Short for Calliope, Calli is a Griot girl (*see Griot*). She is young and intelligent, a free-thinking soul born into slavery who has no record of the date or the place of her birth, or her actual father, mother, or relations. Accustomed to a life of toil, harassment, and humiliation, Calli is a visionary and poet with a unique introspective comprehension of life and her historical experience. Calli is frequently misunderstood by her contemporaries because she lives outside of conventional experience and is an outcast of domestic life. Assisted by Muses, Calli sings and narrates hope for her people. Calli's songs frequently have double meanings, though she speaks truthfully, but metaphorically or prophetically.

Children of children Anyone who strives to make America's leaves of grass greener for its citizens; who has moved beyond their own color to a deeper shade, sharing without bias all the fruits of Democracy: Equality, Justice, Liberty, Truth, Freedom.

Enslaved People either brought to work on plantations by means of the West African slave trade, or those persons born and bred into a condition of slavery, the enslaved are Blacks, but also mulattos and children fathered by slave owners, who are treated like chattel, like property, with no human dignity, living in worse conditions than animals, and treated as evil in order to justify this treatment.

Evalina Wife of Banjo Pete; works in the field; mother of nine children who catch the Freedom train and are always on time; daughter of Maudell Sleet.

Family For the enslaved, family has a broader meaning than the family into which a person is born. A family was composed of any number of individual souls who, having no family of their own, have coalesced into supportive and nurturing surrogate families. Brothers, sisters, mothers, fathers—relationships developed out of an apparent chaos of disoriented and confused slaves who didn't know anybody or communicate in the same language. The family was a natural act of defiance to their enslavers who tried to break the spirit and the will of "their property," and tried to keep slaves from forming any kind of bonds. Family members may not have known where they were born or when, but over time individual identities were renewed in their family, along with dates of birth and names. The family was a saving grace to the constant undermining of self-worth, and physical abuse of slave owners and others attempting to keep slaves from bettering their condition. The parents encouraged children to learn to read and write, though they may not have known how themselves, and the children did not want to disappoint them because it was obvious how hard they worked and how much they gave.

Father Father is a man of truth and humility. He is lean and strong from grueling work in the sun, from dawn to sunset. There are scars on his back from the whip. He knows right from wrong and even under fear of death will not betray his integrity. He treats the women with respect, and challenges the children to outdo what he has done. No child would willingly disappoint the father because of how hard he works and for the courage he shows.

Grandfather Nearly blind and his age unknown, Grandfather sows the seeds of strong mental, physical, and sensitive spirits in the grandchildren. He is compassionate and kind, but he knows from cruel experience the hardships of life, that anything can be borne—even death—which makes him seem a man of infinite patience. Deprived of learning from books, Grandfather loves to study reading and writing. Grandfather knows that the days of youth are not long, and that all are working toward freedom under the sun.

Grandmother Grandmother has raised so many worthy children she knows and has the faith that freedom itself will spill over with them in the time to come. Grandmother passes down to the grandchildren the truth about her God, and she sings God's praise. She is a wise storyteller, and she sings *It's a sweet old story*.

Griot In the tradition of West African storytellers, a Griot is a bard, a wandering singer and musician, a storyteller, whose works are often metaphorical, allegorical, or prophetic. A Griot preserves the history and historical perspective of a culture, and its traditions, or divines their nature and essence and/or reinvents them. A Griot keep the present connected to the past. A Griot preserves a faith in the future.

Miss Claudy Lordy, Lordy Miss Claudy Sings to: DuBois, Garvey, Washington, etc.

Mother Mother is a woman of courage, strength, and an independent spirit that cannot be broken.

She has endured the most bitter of a mother's sorrow: her children taken from her and sold in an auction never to be seen or known again during the days of her life. She defiantly builds new families and communities out of the children who come to her. She is physically strong and can easily do the work that men can do. Mother will never allow the children to think they can't realize their dreams, and pushes her children to overcome, and they do.

Mother Awareness Married to See See Rider; mother of the three Sistas.

Nexus Teenage brother of Angela and Buddy Boy; laying Freedom train's tracks. Buddy Boy and Angela are extremely strong.

Running Boy "I'm gonna run to the city of refuge, I'm gonna run," was written about him by Banjo Pete. He is fitter just to stay one step ahead on account of "paddy rollers." He outruns them on visits he takes to neighboring plantations that they don't ever discover. He may have unnatural talent; at least some call it unfair and he makes the difficult look gracefully easy. Running Boy learned on tracks with no lines or meters and yards, and no time. He has the belief, he knows he can make it there, and is still too young for fear, and no one can stay with him when he runs.

See See Rider Father of Sistas Awareness, Understanding, Insight, and Angela; Prometheus's cousin. Ma Rainey (1886–1939), with See See Rider, was the original role model for a spate of girl Blues shouters.

1. Metaphor for lover or love making. Many metaphors used in the Blues were derived from the process of cooking and other closely related culinary terms. The shade of color of a Black person also played a role: "honey" was

used for a light-skinned person and "coffee" for a deeper shade thus resulting in terms like "honey dripper" and "coffee grinder" as metaphors for a lover. Grinding (coffee in a grinder or wheat in a mill) therefore means having sex.

2. The easy rider, also known as see see rider or c c rider, is a Blues metaphor for the sexual partner. Originally it referred to the guitar hung on the back of the traveling Bluesman. The word "easy" has different meanings for the female and male lover: applied to a woman it is an expression of admiration, but applied to a male it usually carries the meaning of recklessness and unfaithfulness.

3. According to Alex Washburn, "In one of Alan Lomax's folk song collections it says that the abbreviation 'C.C.' means 'Cavalry Corporal,' and that they had no female soldiers at that time (nineteenth century). Now the conclusion from this fact was that the singer or the original songwriter must have been a gay . . . Well, in my opinion, the songwriter even could be a woman singing this song to her soldier lover. Anyway, the author then said that 'C.C. Rider' became 'See See Rider' and 'Easy Rider' because of prudery. . . ." Thanks to Alex Washburn.

4. Southern Louisiana's John "JohnnyB" Bradford says, "An easy rider is the husband or significant other of a whore, thus the name. He doesn't work or pay for sex. It's his easily." Thanks to John "JohnnyB" Bradford for this contribution to the list.

The term "See See Rider" is usually taken as synonymous with "easy rider." In particular, in Blues songs it often refers to a woman who had liberal sexual views, had been married more than once, or was skilled at sex. Although Ma Rainey's version seems on the face of it to refer to "See See Rider" as a man, one theory is that the term refers to a prostitute, and in the lyric "You made me love you, now your man done come," "your man" refers to the woman's pimp. So, rather than being directed to a male "easy rider," the song is in fact an admonition to a prostitute to give up her evil ways.

There are further theories:

· "Easy rider" was sometimes used to refer to the partner of a hypersexual woman, who therefore does not have to work or pay for sex.
· The term was also sometimes used to refer to a slow moving train, as used by itinerant workers in the Great Depression—in particular, it has been suggested, one of the Colorado Central (C.C.) line.
· Another theory is that the term "easy rider" sometimes originally referred to the guitar hung across the back of a travelling Blues singer.
· Other sources indicate that "C.C. Rider" refers to early "Country Circuit" Riding Preachers who traveled on horseback into many towns that were without formal churches at the time. Some of these Circuit Riders had a real reputation as womanizers.

Sista Angela Metaphorical youthful, intelligent, sensitive sista to all the Children of Children; a gifted soulfulizing dancer, performer.

Sista Awareness Daughter of See See Rider; keen perceptions; perspicacity.

Sista Insight Sista Insight is the oldest daughter of See See Rider.

Sista Understanding She is the daughter of See See Rider. Acute sense of the universality of human nature. Hers is the ability to comprehend. Sista Understanding listens attentively to all and prefers to ask the questions. She acquires deeper understanding because she is non-judgmental. She may be approving or disapproving, but she is truthful, and she hears a commonality, and all are drawn together by her ability.

Maudell Sleet Evalina's mother; tends her garden and is a preeminent Griot.

Tellit Tellit, from Shout It Out, Tennessee, a twelve-year-old girl, is the original soul, the idea of a young girl. Unlike a living child of earth, naturally attached to the world and its circumstances, Tellit from this mythical town appears for a moment at Martin Luther King, Jr.'s grave to sing, from an experience somewhere outside of sorrow and loss.

Winfree Free personality; won her freedom. Teaches herself how to read and write. An orphan. Riveting personality, gifted, sings beautiful songs. The soulfulizer that does "I am I am a Black woman."

MISCELLANEOUS

Benjamin Banneker (November 9, 1731–October 9, 1806) The first Black man of science. Calculated first ever survey of the Federal District, now called Washington, D.C. Fascinated by mechanical devices. Took a watch apart at twenty-one. Studied astronomy and his predictions were accurate.

"Diamond" Jim Brady (August 12, 1856–April 13, 1917) This financier and philanthropist was born James Buchanan Brady in New York City to a modest household. Brady worked his way up from bellboy and messenger. After working in the New York Central Railroad system, he became the chief assistant to the general manager by the age of twenty-one. Brady used his knowledge of the railroad industry to become a successful railroad supply salesman. His used his earnings to build an empire of about two million dollars (before he was thirty).

He was known for his love of jewelry, especially diamonds—hence the nickname. He was also known for his enormous girth and appetite. It was not unusual for Brady to eat enough food for ten people at one sitting. A typical Brady breakfast would be eggs, pancakes, pork chops, corn bread, fried potatoes, hominy, muffins, and a beefsteak. For a refreshment, a gallon of orange juice—or "golden nectar," as he called his favorite drink.

Forty acres and a mule Forty acres and a mule is a term for compensation that was promised to be awarded to freed African-American slaves after the Civil War—forty acres of land to farm, and a mule with which to drag a plow so the land could be cultivated.

The award—a land grant of a quarter of a quarter section (one square mile) deeded to heads of households presumably formerly owned by land-holding Whites—was the product of Special Field Orders, No. 15, issued by Maj. Gen. William T. Sherman on January 16, 1865. This award applied to Black families who lived near the coasts of South Carolina, Georgia, and Florida. While there was no actual mention of mules in Sherman's order, the army may have given them out as well. After the assassination of President Abraham Lincoln, his successor, Andrew Johnson, revoked Sherman's orders. About 10,000 freed slaves settled on 400,000 acres in Georgia and South Carolina before President Johnson reversed the order and returned the land to its White former owners. Because of the reversal, the phrase is used as an example of the failure of Reconstruction and the general public to assist African Americans.

Harlem The Black Metropolis. The Technicolor bazaar. A neighborhood in the New York borough of Manhattan, long known as a major Black cultural and business center. The mass migration of Blacks into the area began in 1904, thanks to another real estate crash, the worsening of conditions for Blacks elsewhere in the city, and the leadership of a Black real estate entrepreneur named Philip Payton, Jr. When landlords could not find White renters for their properties, Philip Payton stepped in to bring Blacks. His company, the Afro-American Realty Company, was almost single-handedly responsible for the migration of Blacks from their previous neighborhoods.

Samuel Johnson (September 18 [O.S. September 7], 1709–December 13, 1784) Regularly referred to as Dr. Johnson, he is among England's best known literary figures. Dr. Johnson was an essayist, poet, biographer, lexicographer, and a critic of English literature. Also considered to be a great wit and prose stylist, he was well known for his aphorisms. The single most quoted English writer after Shakespeare, Dr. Johnson has been described as being among the most outstanding figures of eighteenth-century England.

Lewis Howard Latimer (September 4, 1848–December 11, 1928) The architect of the modern light bulb, Latimer was the only Black member of Thomas A. Edison's research team. While Edison invented the incandescent bulb, it was Latimer, a member of the Edison Pioneers, who developed and patented the process for manufacturing the carbon filaments.

Latimer subscribed to the American ideal that any poor boy could make his fame and fortune through invention and innovation. His skills in mechanical drawing landed him a position with Crosby and Gould, patent solicitors. While with the company he advanced to a chief draftsman and soon began working on his own inventions. While working at the Boston firm, Latimer met Alexander Graham Bell, who hired him to draw the plans for a new invention, the telephone.

Jan Matzeliger (September 15, 1852–August 24, 1889) Born in Dutch Guiana (Surinam) to a Dutch engineer father and African mother, he invented a shoe-lasting machine, which would revolutionize shoemaking and reduce the cost of manufacturing.

Elijah McCoy (May 2, 1843–October 10, 1929) McCoy produced more patents than any other Black man, and is responsible for inventing everything from the folding ironing board to the lawn sprinkler. But he was most known for an automatic lubricator for oiling the steam engines of locomotives and boats. Lacking the capital with which to manufacture his lubricators in large numbers, he usually assigned his patent rights to his employers or sold them to investors. Lubricators with the McCoy name were not manufactured until 1920, near the end of his career, when he formed the Elijah McCoy Manufacturing Company. By that time there were several substantial lubricator manufacturers in multiple countries.

Jean Baptiste Pointe du Sable (c. 1745–August 28, 1818) Born in Haiti in 1745. Educated in Paris. Traveled to New Orleans. A trapper along the Mississippi River. Trading post established in Illinois. Built first permanent settlement now called Chicago. Spoke English, Spanish, and French. Sold his Chicago holdings.

Madam CJ Walker (December 23, 1867–May 25, 1919) She became the first female—Black or White—to become a self-made millionaire in the United States, developing and marketing a successful line of beauty and hair products for Black women. Invented a way to soften and smooth Black women's hair.

Born Sarah Breedlove in Delta, Louisiana,

to slaves, she was a washerwoman. After suffering from hair problems, including dandruff and a scalp disease that caused her to go nearly bald, she came up with a formula to help her hair grow. She teamed up with CJ Walker, a newspaperman and a marketer, and took her "Wonderful Hair Grower," on the road. They married and divorced, but Walker kept the name and built an empire.

Walker was also known for her philanthropy, leaving two-thirds of her estate to educational institutions and charities including the NAACP, the Tuskegee Institute, and Bethune-Cookman University. In 1919, her $5,000 pledge to the NAACP's anti-lynching campaign was the largest gift the organization had ever received.

Granville T. Woods (April 23, 1856–January 30, 1910)   Woods had a love of machinery and he invented several items including the telephone transmitter, steam boiler furnace, and railway telegraphy. While he excelled at all that he did, being a Black man during the 1800s meant he was denied many promotions and opportunities. This lead him to form Woods Railway Telegraphy Company in 1884.

Carter G. Woodson (December 19, 1875–April 3, 1950)   He is an important historian, author, and analyst of the twentieth century who was known as the father of Black history. Born a poor son of former slaves, Woodson enrolled in high school at the age of twenty, and in 1912 he became the second African American to earn a Ph.D. from Harvard University (the first was W. E. B. DuBois).

Woodson believed it was important for everyone, especially Blacks, to be aware of how they have influenced culture and history. In 1915, he founded the Association for the Study of Negro Life, and in 1926, Woodson launched Negro History Week, during the second week of February, to celebrate black contributions to the world. This celebration would later evolve into Black History Month.

MUSIC

Marion Anderson (February 27, 1897–April 8, 1993)   An American contralto who received great critical success around the world. However, she was denied the ability to sing to an integrated audience at Constitutional Hall and in the auditorium of a White high school by the District of Columbia because she was Black.

On Easter Sunday in 1939, an open air performance was arranged with the help of First Lady Eleanor Roosevelt on the steps of the Lincoln Memorial in Washington, D.C., for more than 75,000 people in person and millions over the radio to hear Anderson sing.

The Apollo   Also a metaphor. Legendary for its connection to Black and soul music, many of the best known singers and entertainers appeared on its stage. When it opened in 1913 at 125th Street in Harlem, the Apollo Theater featured Black entertainment for White audiences, but in 1934, Sidney Cohen bought the theater and opened the doors to Harlem, "the Technicolor bazaar," and to the Blacks who lived there. In the era before television, during the musical and artistic renaissance on the streets of Harlem, amateur night was a high point of the week. Anyone thinking they had talent could audition and an enthusiastic crowd would cheer them on or boo them off. Bessie Smith, Billie Holiday, Louis Armstrong, and Ella Fitzgerald all won an early amateur night; all the great Black jazz greats came to perform for the crowd at the Apollo. Even those booed went on to fame.

Louis Daniel (Satchmo) Armstrong   (August 4, 1901–July 6, 1971)   Armstrong, also known as Satchmo, is the most famous Black American trumpet player. While he sings and orchestrates as well, his innovative and improvisational style on the trumpet made him famous and beloved. He had a major effect on swing and the big band sound.

Birdland The influential Charlie Parker, "Bird," was the first headliner and gave the club its name. Located near 52nd Street, Birdland was located in the jazz center of New York City in the 1950s and '60s. All the greats played Birdland, including John Coltrane, Dizzy Gillespie, and Miles Davis. The presence of so many jazz giants made the club glamorous, and not only was Birdland the place to hear music but also to be seen with celebrities like Joe Louis and Sugar Ray Robinson.

The Blues The Blues is a form of music that came up out of slavery, from work songs, Baptist spirituals, and the despairs, sorrows, and hopes of the enslaved toiling from sun high to moon low. Using only a few chords but with an infinite number of variations, the Blues was music about being poor and broke, about hard times, about lost love, hopes and dreams, loneliness, and isolation. However, the music is intended to make the listener feel elated because of a shared human experience set to soulful rhythm and melody. Because it works with contradictory human emotions, and sometimes the vital aspects of everyday life, like sex, it is often confused for "the devil's music."

Howlin' Wolf says of the Blues, "When you ain't got no money you got the blues. When you ain't got no money to pay your house rent you still got the blues. When you ain't got no money and can't pay your house rent and can't buy you no food, you damn sure got the blues. Anytime you thinking evil you got the blues."

Blueswomen and Bluesmen Blueswomen and -men play music about how it really is when one day they wake up only to find that everything that they once had is gone, which, as it turns out, is the same uncomfortable situation experienced by every other human being. They play anywhere and anytime—on street corners, in back rooms, at small social gatherings, anywhere where listeners gather to hear about those who have troubles, tragic love affairs, no money and no home, dire circumstances just as bad or maybe a little worse than they do, and because of that to feel strangely reassured that nothing is what it seems.

Ruth Brown (January 12, 1928–November 17, 2006) First mega rhythm and blues singer whose hits made Atlantic Records: "The house that Ruth Brown built." Member of The Hall of Fame; simply one of the best performers of her time.

John Coltrane (September 23, 1926–July 17, 1967) Despite a relatively brief career (he first came to notice as a sideman at age twenty-nine in 1955, formally launched a solo career at thirty-three in 1960, and was dead at forty in 1967). Saxophonist John Coltrane was among the most important, and most controversial, figures in jazz. He reshaped modern jazz and influenced generations of other musicians. Coltrane released about fifty recordings as a leader in those twelve years, and appeared on dozens more led by other musicians.

Miles Davis (May 26, 1926–September 28, 1991) An American jazz trumpeter, Davis was born in a well-to-do family in East St. Louis. He became one of the most influential people in jazz. A local phenom, he toured with Billy Eckstine's band while still in high school. Davis moved to New York under the guise of attending the Juilliard School of Music. However, his real intentions were to hook up with Charlie Parker and Dizzy Gillespie. He became the trumpet player for Charlie Parker's group for nearly three years.

He invented a more subtle, yet still challenging style that became known as "cool jazz." After spending four years fighting a heroin addiction, he conquered it, inspired by the discipline of the boxer Sugar Ray Robinson.

Dixieland In this epic Griot song, Dixieland is a culture where a White has absolute control, and authority over a Black; it's a place where Blacks must use extreme caution; a place to avoid if possible; a place that is more than a geographical division: It's a harsh landscape with multi-subdivisions that shape, with absolute impunity, White misbehavior.

Duke Ellington (April 29, 1899–May 24, 1974) Edward Kennedy Ellington—jazz bandleader, pianist, and composer—was born in Washington, D.C., and is a legendary pioneer in using wordless voices in orchestration. Many jazz greats performed in Ellington's band throughout its long period of popularity. Duke wrote many piano suites, including "Black, Brown, and Beige," "Liberation Suite," "Harlem," and "Blue Bell of Harlem."

Ella Fitzgerald (April 25, 1917–June 15, 1996) Fitzgerald, also known as "Lady Ella" and the "First Lady of Song," is considered one of the most influential jazz vocalists of the twentieth century. She had a vocal range that spanned three octaves and was known for her excellent elocution.

During her career she won thirteen Grammy Awards, was awarded the National Medal of Art by Ronald Reagan, the Presidential Medal of Freedom by George H. W. Bush, and sold over 40 million albums.

Dizzy Gillespie (October 21, 1917–January 6, 1993) John Birks "Dizzy" Gillespie was born in Cheraw, South Carolina. During the early 1940s, he and Charlie "Yardbird" Parker virtually reinvented jazz as bop or bebop. A gifted trumpet innovator, bandleader, and a musical provocateur—a Griot: a soulfull performer who colors moment to moment with humanity's universal song.

Milt Hinton (June 23, 1910–December 19, 2000) Milt Hinton is regarded as one of the greatest jazz bassists of all time. He has been nicknamed "The Judge" for his outstanding musical ability. He possessed a formidable technique and was equally adept at bowing, pizzicato, and "slapping," a technique for which he became famous while playing with the big band of Cab Calloway in the 1930s. Unusual for a double bass player, Hinton was frequently given the spotlight by Calloway, taking virtuosic bass solos.

Also a fine photographer, Hinton documented many of the great jazz musicians via photographs he took over the course of his career. Milt Hinton was one of the best friends of the great jazz trumpeter Louis Armstrong.

Billie Holiday (April 7, 1915–July 17, 1959) Born Elenora Fagan, fourteen-year-old Holiday moved to Harlem, New York City, with her mother in 1929. The two lived in a brothel, before Holiday was picked up by the police and sent to Welfare Island on the East River. After her release, she began to sing at rent parties and in small Harlem clubs for coins patrons would throw at her feet. She gave herself the stage name Billie Holiday, which she half borrowed from Billie Dove, a 1920s starlet who played the damsel in distress, and Clarence Holiday, her runaway father. However, she was also known by her fans and band by the name "Lady Day."

In 1933, she was discovered by the well-known music critic, John Hammond, and her musical career began to flower. She had a haunting, lyrical sound and was able to sell millions of albums. Her song "Strange Fruit," originally a poem about a lynching, drew the attention of the FBI, which opened a file on Billie as a potential agitator.

In 1947, at the height of her fame, she was jailed on drug charges and served an eight-month prison sentence in West Virginia. For her crime, she was barred from working in clubs the rest of her life. She died at the age of forty-four with only a few hundred dollars to her name. Billie is now regarded as one of the most important female vocalists in the history of jazz.

Howlin' Wolf (June 10, 1910–January 10, 1976) His grandfather would tell Chester Arthur Burnett stories about wolves to keep him out of trouble, but Burnett got so worked up about doing wrong he would howl himself, and so he became "Howlin' Wolf." Wolf was born just off the highway between West Point and Aberdeen, Mississippi. He did the hard labor on the poor family farm in Mississippi. At eighteen his father gave him a guitar and Wolf began playing on the street. During his travels he met Charley Patton, a famous rambler and Blues guitarist, who showed Wolf how to play Delta Blues. Wolf went on to develop a reputation with fellow musicians as one of the greatest slide guitar players.

He served in short term in World War II before returning to work on his father's farm in Arkansas. However, his big break came when he landed a weekly show on a Memphis radio station and sang in local juke joints on the side. With his deep-chest growling voice he'd punctuate his remarks and his music with howls. He became very successful and was a significant influence on the major British rhythm and blues bands of early 1960s, including the Rolling Stones and Eric Clapton.

Mahalia Jackson (October 26, 1911–January 27, 1972) Known as the "Queen of the Gos-pel Song," Jackson was born in New Orleans, Louisiana. As the daughter of a barber-stevedore-preacher, she sang in her father's choir. At sixteen Jackson moved to Chicago, Illinois, where she became a member of Greater Salem Baptist Church and eventually its soloist. She began recording gospel music and enjoyed increasing popularity in the South. Her single "Move On Up a Little Higher" sold more than a million copies, and with it came nationwide attention. During her career she recorded about thirty albums, mostly on Columbia Records, and several sold over a million copies.

Jazz At first jazz was jass, a type of music born in the late 1800s that was named after the jasmine perfume worn by prostitutes in Storyville, New Orleans. Jazz emerged from the different influences arriving from overseas and flooding downriver from inland America, jumbled together in New Orleans, a thriving seaport town. African, Caribbean, European, all contributed their languages, art, and music. Baptist spirituals, the Blues, classical, horns and brass bands, but the all-important ingredient was the creative energy brought by freed former slaves and the elation of new-found freedom.

For the slave, music had been a means of solace, improvised in the fields during work, to express the deepest emotions, the pain of hard labor, the grief of death and parting, spiritual yearnings, every aspect of life. Jazz used the same improvisational technique but with instruments finding their own voice, yet blending harmoniously with the band.

When the Jim Crow system began in 1877, jazz migrated out of New Orleans to the major American cities, Chicago and New York, and the great musicians of the era followed it on its journey. Jazz played with elegance and style remained unbashful about human flaws and imperfections like the life in Storyville.

Robert Johnson (May 8, 1911–August 16, 1938) Robert Johnson is one of the most famous of the Delta Blues (music from Mississippi Delta) musicians. By all accounts and the legacy of his recordings he was a young man of gifted intelligence who died at twenty-seven. His landmark recordings from 1936 to 1937 display a remarkable combination of singing, guitar skills and songwriting talent that have influenced generations of musicians.

Lead Belly (January 1888–December 6, 1949) Born Huddie William Ledbetter, Lead Belly got his name being a "lead" and companion for a blind Blues musician, Blind Lemon Jefferson, who died years later in Chicago when he wandered off into a snow storm. Lead Belly left home at twenty and explored the back roads of the southwest, picking up work songs, playing guitar where he could, and working as a laborer. He had a temper, which landed him in prison twice for attempted murder. The first time was in Texas during 1917, but he was pardoned by the governor, and then in 1930, after a fight at a party, thanks to Jim Crow South. This time he was freed with the help of two well-known musicologists, John and Alan Lomax, who were recording prison songs for the Library of Congress. In gratitude Lead Belly worked as their chauffeur in New York when he was released.

Lead Belly came to resent any reference to his being a convict, but life in Southern prisons contributed to his repertoire of spirituals, Blues songs, field songs, and children's songs. Lead Belly became "King of The Twelve-String Guitar," and in a strong voice demanding attention belted out road crew work songs, and songs about life on death row and the gallows. He developed a repertoire of several hundred songs and made many recordings that endure to the present day. His songs were a natural at political rallies and union gatherings.

Ma Rainey (April 26, 1886–December 22, 1939) Early Blues singer, now called "The Mother of the Blues," was born Gertrude Malissa Nix Pridgett in Columbus, Georgia. She married actor William (Pa) Rainey, and during the early 1920s she began recording. By 1929 she had numerous successful recordings.

Big Maybelle (May 1, 1924–January 23, 1972) Born Maybelle Louise Smith in Jackson, Tennessee. At eight she was talented and precocious enough to win top honors in a Memphis amateur contest. When Maybelle was discovered by producer Fred Mendelsohn he signed her to a Columbia Okeh R&B subsidiary and changed her name to Big Maybelle. Today she is known as a premier rhythm and blues giant with a deep gravelly voice.

Charlie Parker (August 29, 1920–March 12, 1955) An American jazz saxophonist and composer, Parker is considered one of the pioneers of jazz along with Louis Armstrong and Duke Ellington. Known as "Yardbird," or "Bird," Parker played a leading role in the development of bebop, a form of jazz characterized by fast tempos, virtuoso technique, and improvisation based on harmonic structure. Parker's innovative approaches to melody, rhythm, and harmony exercised enormous influence on his contemporaries.

Bessie Smith (July 9, 1892 or April 15, 1894–September 26, 1937) Born in Chattanooga, Tennessee, Bessie's parents passed away by the time she was nine and care of the family fell to a sister. Bessie became a street performer in Chattanooga, where she and her brother sang and danced for pennies to hold off the poverty. In 1912, she joined a show featuring Pa and Ma Rainey. Ma, eight years Bessie's senior and established in show business, the "Mother of the Blues," showed Bessie life in the business. Bessie sang hypnotic blues, and with soulful pride about everyday troubles so that everybody heard what she was singing about, but only Bessie told the story how it ought to be told. Bessie became the "Empress of the Blues."

She made recordings during the era of "race records," records made by Blacks and meant for Black audiences. Now her recordings are treasured collector's items, and played until the needle has nearly worn through the vinyl. Bessie was so popular she received a roll in a short movie, *St. Louis Blues*, which featured a prohibition speakeasy.

Bessie was intolerant of racism and once stood up to the Ku Klux Klan. The Klan surrounded a tent where she was performing in a small town in North Carolina in July 1927. Nonplussed, Bessie confronted the troublemakers and said she'd bring the entire audience after them so "you had better pick up them sheets and run!" They did and Smith returned to the bandstand.

Bessie died after a tragic auto accident in Memphis. She died in an ambulance in transit to a "colored hospital" and not the closest hospital to the car wreck, giving her death an aura of controversy, now considered to be untrue. Her grave was unmarked until 1970, when a new generation of fans purchased a monument for her.

Kate Smith (May 1, 1907–June 17, 1986) American singer best known for her rendition of Irving Berlin's "God Bless America." Smith had a radio, television, and recording career spanning five decades, reaching its most-remembered zenith in the 1940s.

Billy Strayhorn (November 29, 1915–May 31, 1967) Born William Thomas "Billy" Strayhorn, in Dayton, Ohio, he was a composer, pianist, and arranger. He was best known for his two-decade musical partnership with the great Duke Ellington. Together they composed and arranged music that showcased, in the best performing light, the talent and personality of band members. Duke said, "Billy is my left arm, my right arm, all the eyes in the back of my head, my brain . . . his brain is mine." Billy's gifts live today in his music.

Sarah Vaughan (March 27, 1924–April 3, 1990) Affectionately known as "Sassy" and "The Divine Sarah," Sarah Vaughan is undoubtedly one of the greatest jazz singers of all time. She has won three Grammy Awards and the National Endowment for the Arts bestowed upon her its highest honor in jazz, the NEA Jazz Masters Award, in 1989.

Dinah Washington (August 29, 1924–December 14, 1963) Queen of the blues. Born Ruth Lee Jones. As a child she moved from Tuscaloosa, Alabama, to Chicago, Illinois. There she played the piano and directed the choir. At sixteen she toured the Black Gospel circuit. She was an extraordinary talent who died at the age of thirty-nine.

Ben Webster (March 27, 1909–September 20, 1973) Known as the "Brute" or "The Frog," this jazz saxophonist was considered one of three of the most important swing tenors along with Lester Young and Coleman Hawkins.

Lester Young (August 27, 1909–March 15, 1959) Nicknamed "Prez," he was an American tenor saxophonist and clarinetist. Young, a jazz legend, began his career as a member of Count Basie's band.

MYTH AND RELIGION

Abel Abel was the second son of Adam and Eve and the brother of Cain. Abel was murdered by Cain and was the first martyr in the Bible.

Apollo The sun god and leader of the Muses, the director of their choir, god of music and poetry, and of oracles and of the prophets.

Cain The first son of Adam and Eve and Abel's brother. Cain was a farmer who violated the will of God by killing his brother, Abel, a shepherd, in the first act of murder recounted in the Bible.

Christianity When slaves found themselves captives in a foreign land, they brought their own gods and faith, but were forbidden to gather and worship on their own. They had to meet in secret and were punished if they were found out. Enslavers began to use Christianity to promote docility, and to prevent uprisings and being murdered at the hands of their own slaves. But the slave would not accept a system that deprived them of personal liberty, subjected them to humiliation and torture, and promised salvation in an afterlife, while "masters" were entitled to paradise on earth. Although many Christian ministers and preachers could not reconcile slavery with Christianity, many overcame their aversion to slavery for the sake of profit, or became convinced that slavery was a beneficial system, so Christianity was sometimes two-faced toward slavery.

As time separated the enslaved from their past, and new generations were born, different elements and stories in Christianity were admired as metaphors of the human experience, and were borrowed and blended with the spirituality of African traditions. Stories in the Bible became personal and not Christian morality tales promoting obedience. Stories like Moses crossing into the Promised Land, for example, were emblematic confirmation that liberty was "just beyond the river," that it is a Christian responsibility to make the effort to cross over, not an act of disobedience to a human master.

The early years of the American Republic occurred simultaneously with the period of Enlightenment, and philosophies of human individuality and freedom made their way into the new American democracy, and these theories about life, liberty, and the pursuit of happiness, also found their way into Christianity. In movements like "The Great Awakening," a new way of believing was preached by free-thinking ministers. God was no longer the sole property of philosophers, and the established religious order, but belonged as well to the common people and the slave.

David David began life as a shepherd and grew to become a great king. When he was a boy David showed great courage when he defeated Goliath, a Philistine giant, with a slingshot. David also wrote the psalms, and Jesus was one of his descendents.

Ethos Sentiment and feeling, ethos is the persuasive power exerted upon the minds and hearts of the observers and witnesses of a play or an event, or a scene, or a speaker, which causes an audience to believe and trust and to become sympathetically disposed toward the actors and speakers, and then brings forth in this audience a friendly, favorable, and trusting response.

Fate Fate puts mortals into unavoidable predicaments and circumstances, "fates," over the course of human life. There are forks along the route, and there are inevitabilities that involve no act of choosing. The acquiring of wisdom is greatly attributable to the acts of fate shaping and helping to determine individual experience. Riches, fame, or poverty may be deleterious or wrong decisions. Fate helps shape human history through every living being.

Gabriel Gabriel "stands in the presence of God," and is an archangel who serves as one of God's chief messengers. According to legend, he is the unidentified angel in the Book of Revelations who blows the horn announcing Judgment Day.

God Three hundred and sixty degrees in every direction, God has a center, which is everywhere and has no boundaries. Only God knows the true nature of every being. God works behind or within the scenes so subtly it is difficult to discern where nature ends and God begins. God is a mysterious and illusive truth and goodness whose justice is as great for those afflicted by a wrongful idea as for those who suffer by it. Despite rumors, God is as concerned for the welfare of the very least as for the high and mighty, and for whom skin color is irrelevant. Although God supports the poor and the afflicted, it is the responsibility of human beings to fight the inequities of rotted governmental systems. When God intervenes in human affairs the action is performed so subtly and occurs at such a natural pace, that it is difficult to interpret as intervention except for a favoring in the balance of justice, leading many to lament that life is a pitiful state, spent yearning that if God sustains nature, God should do so without ambiguity, but this is representative of human pride.

Goliath Goliath was a great Philistine warrior of huge proportions who challenged the Israelites to send a warrior of their own to challenge him in battle. David came forward and, using only a rock and a sling, killed Goliath.

Heavenly Father *See God.*

Holy Ghost God's nonvisible spirit that permeates and sustains all that can be seen with the eyes, and an essence, which is known in the reflection of the soul, by which it is dimly possible for mortals to make out the likeness of divine truth.

Mary Mary is the mother of Christ. Mary is an exemplary mother because she had faith that her child was a gift of God, though she and her husband lived in poverty and suffered the worst sort of human tyranny. Mary trusted God's promise that her child would bring hope and be a prophet, and her faith was rewarded.

Orpheus Orpheus was the son of Calliope and Apollo. His musical and poetic talents were so great that he could charm the birds out of the trees, and perform other magical acts.

Orpheus's wife, Eurydice, was killed by the bite of a serpent, and Orpheus went to the underworld to work his magical abilities there and bring her back. His songs were so beautiful that he succeeded. But he was warned not to look over his shoulder on the return to the surface or Eurydice would not be allowed to leave the underworld. Just before Orpheus reached the world, he looked back, and Eurydice was lost again.

Pathos Pathos is that form of emotional persuasion by which one endeavors to put their audience into whatever frame of mind is favorable to one's purpose.

Prometheus Prometheus is considered by many to be one of the original heroic gods. It was Prometheus who stole the practical arts, which were the property of the gods, and gave them to humankind. Prometheus did this because alone among the gods he had compassion for the wretched and exposed condition of the humans who inhabited the world.

The practical arts were necessities like fire, for which he is well known, but also woodworking and masonry, and knowledge of the stars for navigation, the numbers and the alphabet, divination, and art. It was theft because Zeus forbade that humans have any of these necessities. When Zeus discovered the deception, he chained Prometheus to a rock where an eagle tore at his flesh, but in time Prometheus was freed.

River Jordan Supplies Israel and Jordan with vast amounts of their water.

Sisyphus Deceitful in life, punished for robbery and fraud, cursed to roll a rock uphill, which on arriving promptly rolls back to the bottom over and over again throughout eternity.

The Upper Room The Upper Room was located in an unknown house in Jerusalem where Jesus reclined with his disciples for a last meal, the Passover. But the Upper Room represents any place or state of mind where a spiritually minded individual can contemplate God without interruption or distraction. In the Upper Room, disciples taking one step in the direction of God are visited by the Holy Spirit taking two steps in theirs.

RELIGIOUS

George Baker (aka Father Divine) (c. 1880–September 10, 1965) Baker was also known as Father Divine, an African-American spiritual leader from about 1907 until his death. His full self-given name was Reverend Major Jealous Divine, and he was also known as "the Messenger." He founded the International Peace Mission movement, formulated its doctrine, and oversaw its growth from a small and predominantly Black congregation into a multiracial and international church. Controversially, Father Divine claimed to be God. Some contemporary critics also claimed he was a charlatan, and some suppose him to be one of the first modern cult leaders. However, Father Divine made numerous contributions toward his followers' economic independence and racial equality.

Daddy Grace (January 25, 1884–January 12, 1960) Bishop C. M. Grace, known to his followers as Sweet Daddy Grace, came to America from Portugal in 1903, and settled in New Bedford, Massachusetts. He founded, built, and organized the United House of Prayer for All People. To his followers he was a spiritual leader, counselor, and father, and they affectionately called him "Daddy." Later, in 1919, he built the first House of Prayer in West Wareham, Massachusetts. The flamboyant bishop was an effective evangelist who preached revival in a Pentecostal tradition that included brass "shout bands" and public baptisms.

The United House of Prayer for All People has an ecstatic worship style that includes speaking in tongues. By the time of his death in 1960, Daddy Grace had become a rich man. The church he founded had about 3.5 million members and headquarters in Washington, D.C.

Lemuel Haynes (July 18, 1754–September 28, 1833) Haynes's African father and his mother, the daughter of a socially prominent White family, abandoned him shortly after birth and bound him to indentured servitude until he was twenty-one. Once free, he enlisted as a minuteman in the local militia and fought in the American Revolution. During his enlistment he wrote a ballad-sermon about the Battle of Lexington in 1775.

Haynes was an avid reader of the Bible and books on theology. Following the war, Haynes studied Latin and Greek, and in 1780 was licensed to preach and ordained as a minister. Haynes had three pastorates after his ordination. During his second pastorate, Haynes earned an international reputation as a preacher and writer, and in 1804 received an honorary master of arts degree from Middlebury College, the first ever bestowed upon an African American. He was also the first Black man to serve as a pastor to an all-White congregation.

PRESIDENTS AND GOVERNMENT

The Bill of Rights In the United States, the Bill of Rights is the name that incorporates the first ten amendments to the United States Constitution. They were introduced by James Madison to the First United States Congress in 1789 as a series of constitutional amendments, and came into effect on December 15, 1791, when they had been ratified by three-fourths of the states.

Salmon P. Chase (January 13, 1808–May 7, 1873) Chase was a politician and jurist in the Civil War era who held several political offices including United States senator, governor, United States treasury secretary, and chief justice of the United States. He devoted his energies to the destruction of what he considered the slave power—the conspiracy of Southern slave owners to seize control of the federal government and block the progress of liberty.

Chase articulated the "Slave Power conspiracy" thesis well before Lincoln did, and he coined the slogan of the Free Soil Party, "Free Soil, Free Labor, Free Men."

The Constitution It was adopted on September 17, 1787, by the Constitutional Convention in Philadelphia, Pennsylvania, and later ratified by conventions in each state in the name of "The People"; it has since been amended twenty-seven times. The first ten amendments are known as the Bill of Rights. The Articles of Confederation and Perpetual Union was actually the first constitution of the United States of America. The United States Constitution replaced the Articles of Confederation as the governing document for the United States. It is the supreme law of the United States of America. It provides the framework for the organization of the United States Government. The document outlines the three main branches of the government: executive, legislative, and judicial.

Orville Faubus (January 7, 1910–December 14, 1994) He was a six-term Democratic governor of Arkansas, having served from 1955 to 1967. He is best known for his 1957 stand against the desegregation of Little Rock public schools during the Little Rock Crisis, in which he defied a unanimous decision of the United States Supreme Court by ordering the Arkansas National Guard to stop African-American students from attending Little Rock Central High School. Despite his initial staunch segregationist stance, Faubus much later moderated his positions. He even endorsed the African-American minister Jesse Jackson in the 1984 Democratic presidential primaries.

Freedman's bank Congress passed the Act of Incorporation for the Freedman's Savings and Trust Company and President Lincoln signed it into law on March 3, 1865. The Savings and Trust Company was chartered by Congress for the enhancement of the newly freed slaves to teach them to save money for the future, to be thrifty, and to be productive. The objective of the Savings and Trust Company was straightforward and clear. It was suppose to be a direct path to economic stability for the negro. Although the bank got off to a promising start, by March 1874, when Frederick Douglass became its president, it was on the verge of failure.

Government An established system of administration that manages states, nations, and countries.

Ulysses S. Grant (April 27, 1822–July 23, 1885) He was the eighteenth president of the United States of America. He achieved international fame as the leading Union general in the

American Civil War. Grant first reached national prominence by taking forts Henry and Donelson in 1862 in the first Union victories of the war.

Andrew Johnson (December 29, 1808–July 31, 1875) He was the seventeenth president of the United States of America, succeeding to the presidency upon the assassination of Abraham Lincoln. Johnson was a senator from Tennessee, and was the only Southern senator not to quit his post upon succession, thus becoming the most prominent Democrat from the South supporting the policies of Lincoln.

Lyndon B. Johnson (August 27, 1908–January 22, 1973) The thirty-sixth president of the United States of America, succeeded John F. Kennedy after his assassination. Johnson, from Texas, was a major leader of the Democratic Party and as president was responsible for designing the "Great Society" legislation that included civil rights laws, Medicare (health care for the elderly), Medicaid (health care for the poor), aid to education, and the "War on Poverty." Simultaneously, he escalated the American involvement in the Vietnam War, which from went from 16,000 soldiers to 550,000 in early 1968.

John Fitzgerald "Jack" Kennedy (May 29, 1917–November 22, 1963) He was the thirty-fifth president of the United States of America, the youngest man in history elected to the highest office. He is also the only president to have won a Pulitzer Prize and the only practicing Roman Catholic to be president. Events during his administration include the Bay of Pigs Invasion, the Cuban Missile Crisis, the building of the Berlin Wall, the Space Race, the African-American Civil Rights Movement, and early events of the Vietnam War.

Kennedy was assassinated on November 22, 1963, in Dallas, Texas. Lee Harvey Oswald was charged with the crime and was murdered two days later by Jack Ruby before he could be put on trial. The Warren Commission concluded that Oswald had acted alone in killing the president; however, the House Select Committee on Assassinations declared in 1979 that there was more likely a conspiracy that included Oswald. The entire subject remains controversial, with multiple theories about the assassination still being debated.

Abraham Lincoln (February 12, 1809–April 15, 1865) The sixteenth president of the United States of America. Lincoln won the Republican Party nomination in 1860, and was elected president later that year. During his term, he helped preserve the United States by leading the defeat of the secessionist Confederate States of America in the American Civil War. He introduced measures that resulted in the abolition of slavery, issuing his Emancipation Proclamation in 1863 and promoting the passage of the Thirteenth Amendment to the Constitution, which passed Congress before Lincoln's death and was ratified by the states later in 1865. He was the first president in U.S. history to be assassinated, in 1865 by John Wilkes Booth, which made him a martyr for the ideal of national unity.

Promissory notes An effective palliative used to seduce Black citizens' behavior and expectations by promising all those emancipated forty acres and a mule.

Supreme Court of the United States of America The nation's highest ruling law court that continually monitors and rules on what's Constitutional to all served sitting at America's grand tables.

Herman Talmadge (August 9, 1913–March 21, 2002) Talmadge was a Democratic governor and senator in the state of Georgia. He was also a staunch opponent of civil rights legislation at the height of the civil rights movement.

George Washington (February 22, 1732–December 14, 1799)   The first president of the United States of America, who led the Continental Army to victory over the empire of Great Britain in the American Revolutionary War.

George Wallace (August 25, 1919–September 13, 1998)   He was elected governor of Alabama as a Democrat for four terms (1963–1967, 1971–1979, and 1983–1987), and ran for United States president four times, running as a Democrat in 1964, 1972, and 1976, and as the American Independent Party candidate in 1968. He is best known for his pro-segregation attitudes and as being a symbol of bigotry during the American desegregation period, which he modified after the passage of the 1964 Civil Rights Act.

Wallace became a born-again Christian in the late 1970s and apologized for his earlier segregationist views to Black civil rights leaders.

SLAVERY: PRE- AND POST-CIVIL WAR

Black Code (1863–1877)   During the years of Southern Reconstruction, Confederates established Black Codes which determined and enforced "acceptable" behavior for the newly freed Blacks. The Black Codes also prevented Blacks from owning their own property, effectively keeping Blacks in poverty, and where it created serfdom as an acceptable substitute for the ownership of slaves.

Bossman   Satirical and mildly deprecatory expression used by Blacks, although not understood as such by the bossman. Used to address slave owners and any law enforcement officer, bus driver, or any other person who enforced Jim Crow.

Conductors   Conductors were guides on the Underground Railroad. They came from various backgrounds, and included former slaves, free-born Blacks, Northern abolitionists, and people familiar with the lay of the land and the way north, or those willing to protect or house escaped slaves on their journey. At the start, a brave Conductor, risking his life, would arrive at a Southern plantation, perhaps disguised as a slave, and organize those willing to make the escape. At secretive times, in the night, or in the dead of winter, the Conductor would lead these groups or individuals out of slavery, or deliver them safely to other Conductors on the route.

Crows   Slang for any person who enforced Jim Crow laws and rules of behavior. From bus drivers who enforced segregated seating on public transportation, to mayors and law enforcement officers that supported Jim Crow laws and etiquette with violence or imprisonment.

Democracy   Democracy is a system of "people power," of government by the people and for the people, which grants equality to all of its citizens and the freedom to think for one's self and to live according to one's own free will. This inalienable right is upheld directly by citizens of a democracy, or by representatives freely elected by the people.

Dixie Land   Dixie Land is an expression which refers to the eleven Southern states that seceded from the Union and formed the Confederate States of America just prior to the Civil War—South Carolina, Mississippi, Florida, Alabama, Georgia, Louisiana, Texas, Virginia, Arkansas, North Carolina and Tennessee.

The Drinking Gourd   The Drinking Gourd is another name for the Big Dipper, and the stars in the handle of the Gourd point to the North Star. Escaping slaves, Conductors, and passengers on the Underground Railroad were able to navigate by following the Drinking Gourd. Conductors and passengers or anyone navigating their way out of the South, would sing the following song:

> When the sun comes back and the first quail calls,
> Follow the drinking gourd,
> For the old man is waiting to carry you to freedom
> If you follow the drinking gourd.

The Emancipation Proclamation President Abraham Lincoln issued The Emancipation Proclamation on December 31, 1862, giving all slaves in areas not held by Union troops, and in the Confederate States, their freedom. Prior to the Proclamation, the Civil War had been a war fought to preserve the Union, to prevent the secession of the Confederate States. After the Proclamation, the war was transformed into a war to abolish slavery. On hearing news of the Proclamation, slaves on Southern plantations realized that their individual and collective freedom was dependent on the outcome of the war. After the Proclamation over 200,000 Black soldiers were permitted to join the Union army, which helped the Union army and navy establish a military superiority.

Freedom "Freedom" is a word always open to interpretation, and a human condition is a state of constant change and reorganization. In part freedom means the right to live and think as one chooses, in a rational manner and respectful that a human being would treat others as he or she would wish to be treated themselves—the first credo of many religions. Freedom is the right to be left alone, to be able to wander the roads, or to belong to a community according to a person's free will.

Freedom Fighter Freedom fighters were Black soldiers who fought during the Civil War. They also fought during the War of Independence. Any Black or White who takes a stand against oppression and unreasonable violence is a freedom fighter. A freedom fighter might fight with nonviolence as did Martin Luther King, Jr., but when the time comes a freedom fighter will put his or her life on the line for the cause, like Harriet Tubman, or John Brown. Not just dramatic figures in Black history, but also the actions of anyone great or small who challenged the authority of slave owners, or the KKK (Bessie Smith, who single-handedly challenged the KKK at one of her performances), of Jim Crow, of racial inequality in America. Freedom fighters fight for equitable change, even if that change does not come in the course of a lifetime.

The Great Migration Beginning in 1910 and through the 1940s, thousands of Blacks packed up and left the South and its Jim Crow laws, the violence and segregation, and the remnants of slavery. This exodus became known as the Great Migration. Southern Black workers left for the new Northern industrial jobs, and talented Black musicians traveled to Northern and Midwestern cities for an opportunity to create jazz. They left behind the oppression of the South for better education, the right to vote in free elections, and the hope of life without violence.

Jim Crow (1876–1965) The expression "Jim Crow" dates back to a piece of minstrel music written and performed by a White man in blackface about a farm hand, Jim Crow. "Jim Crow" became the term used for both new laws and a demeaning set of behavioral standards following the end of Reconstruction, replacing the "Black Codes" that preceded them. The Jim Crow laws and codes practically reversed all the gains that free Blacks had made during Reconstruction. Blacks were once again treated like a lower order of beings, and this inferiority was enforced with laws that denied Blacks public transportation or relegated them to the back seats of buses and trains, separate public facilities were enforced, and Blacks couldn't eat in White restaurants. Blacks were denied equal opportunity in jobs and the right to live in White neighborhoods and attend White schools. The Jim Crow codes determined that Black people had to address White people in a certain way, like Ma'am or Sir, and couldn't look White people in the eyes, but had to keep their head down deferentially. If a Black man seemed to address a White woman improperly, it might mean being lynched. Many Blacks and their families were harassed, beaten, or lynched as a result of the Jim Crow laws and this persisted until the Civil Rights movement in the 1960s, prolonging the aftermath of the Civil War for an additional century.

Jubilee (April 9, 1865) This was the day when the Civil War ended. On that day, millions of Blacks crossed the line from two hundred years of enslavement into a freedom that most had never before experienced in their lives. Although Blacks technically remained enslaved until December 6, 1865, eight months after the end of hostilities when the Thirteenth Amendment to the Constitution was ratified, nevertheless, April 9 was the day of Jubilee, a day of rejoicing.

Ku Klux Klan Once claiming over five million members, at its peak the Ku Klux Klan (KKK) conducted an average of two lynchings a week. The KKK originally emerged at the end of the Civil War. Defeated Confederate soldiers organized militias to resist a way of life which they felt was being imposed upon them, and to which they believed they were incapable of adapting. Wearing robes and masks, the KKK set fire to newly constructed schools and churches, and murdered and lynched Blacks. Although President Ulysses S. Grant was able to substantially break the KKK by 1872, the Klan reappeared during the time of the Great Migration, and then again in the 1950s and during the Civil Rights Movement.

The Mason-Dixon Line The Mason-Dixon Line (or "Mason and Dixon's Line") is a boundary between four U.S. states, formed by the borders of Pennsylvania, Maryland, Delaware, and West Virginia (then part of Virginia). Popular speech, especially since the Missouri compromise of 1820 (apparently the first official usage of the term "Mason and Dixon's Line"), uses the Mason-Dixon Line symbolically as a cultural boundary between the northern United States and the southern United States (Dixie).

Patrollers Patrollers were "paddy rollers"—men with whips, hunting dogs, and firearms—that roamed the road between Southern plantations and farms preventing slaves from running away, or chasing after those who had. To the slave owner, a member of the "Slaveocracy," a slave was personal property. If one of his slaves were to escape, he felt it was his Constitutional right to go and get his property back. Escapes occurred so frequently that slave owners organized patrols to hunt down fugitive slaves. Patrollers ordered slaves on the open road or any Blacks they felt looked suspicions, to show identification papers. Passes identified the Black slave, where they were from, and listed distinguishing features. Patrollers returned slaves to the plantations for rewards. If captured by a patroller, a slave would be whipped or beaten or sometimes put to death on his return.

Reconstruction Reconstruction was the period following the end of the Civil War until 1877. During these years, federal troops stayed in the former Confederate states to preserve the peace and to defend the new amendments to the Constitution, giving many rights to freed Blacks. It was a time of great promise, and schools were constructed, Blacks were given the right to vote, and many were elected to public office. However, in 1877, Reconstruction was derailed when Rutherford Hayes withdrew federal troops from the territories and many of the gains that were made were violently reversed by Southerners reluctant to accept change.

Slavery Slavery could be found in America even in the very earliest settlements during the 1600s. Portuguese sailors captured Africans in cargo holds along the trade winds west to the Caribbean, and then north up the coast of America, where they were sold to colonialists seeking free labor to tame their new world. Some Africans would throw themselves into the ocean and drown rather than be taken into captivity. Those captured were chained together and crowded into ships like cattle, where they often sickened and died. When they did die, they were thrown overboard to the sharks following in the ship's wake.

Those who survived the journey to America, millions of African men, women, and children, were auctioned off, and put to work on farms and plantations. If they resisted, slaves were beaten, stripped, and tied to posts on the ground and whipped. When the whipping was done, brine was thrown on the wounds of both men and women alike.

A master would often treat his slaves worse than the meanest animal. Slaves were kept in ignorance, deprived of learning, of reading and writing, of religion, and of their culture and history in order to maintain the dominance of the slave owner. Slaves were housed in small cabins and children were sometimes fed from troughs. Just enough food was provided for survival, and men, women, and children worked the fields half clothed and often until their only pair of shoes were worn out and they walked in their bare feet.

A slave might be sold at any time in an auction, and separated from children, mothers, fathers, and loved ones, never to see each other again during the course of their lives. Their sorrow would be treated with derision by their masters to enforce further subservience, but slaves continually ran and rebelled. Slave owners pursued and punished them to maintain their way of life and the fortunes made through farming and low-cost slave labor, and to mitigate fears of reprisal at the hands of mistreated human beings.

Underground Railroad The Underground Railroad was a secret transportation system on which slaves would catch a ride to freedom in the years prior to the Civil War. Not actually a railroad, but a network of footpaths, roads, and sometimes trains, boats, rivers, and waterways by which, with a "conductor" to guide them, slaves escaped to freedom in the North and Canada. Plantation slaves would relay departure times and itineraries through the grapevine. Because of the secretive nature of the Railroad, when time for escape arrived, Black slaves would alert each other by singing "code" tunes, songs about traveling to the Promised Land or the "Drinking Gourd." (*See Drinking Gourd.*) Along the route were "stations" where escaping slaves would rest, and abolitionists, Quakers, friends, and "stationmasters" would assist them with a place to stay, or financially, or with food and clothing. Often wading neck deep across rivers, or bushwhacking through woods and thickets, traveling at night or in the dead of winter, fleeing slaves took a great risk leaving a familiar life, any kind of meals, a place to live, family and friends, all to escape to the unknown. On the run from the slave owner, and living in fear of patrollers, mercenaries, and informants, escaping slaves captured on the Railroad faced being returned to the plantation, a violent beating, or death.

SPORTS

Jim Brown (February 17, 1936–) James Nathaniel "Jim" Brown played for the Cleveland Browns from 1957 to 1965, and is regarded as the best running back of all time. He is also considered to be the best lacrosse player in the history of the game playing at Syracuse University. In 1957, in the final game of his Syracuse lacrosse career, Brown scored five goals in half a game of play in the Collegiate All-Star game. Playing professional football for the Cleveland Browns, Brown ran over a 1,000 yards in every year of his career but one, and in 1963 Brown became the first running back to run for more than a mile with a total of 1,863 yards. He is remembered for his power, quickness, and resiliency. After being tackled, he would slowly pick himself up off the field and in the following play, run for the same yardage all over again, down after down.

Brown acted in more than thirty movies such as *Ice Station Zebra* and *The Dirty Dozen*, and he is in the hall of fame in both football and lacrosse. Brown has been called the greatest athlete of all time.

Wilt Chamberlain (August 21, 1936–October 12, 1999)   "The Big Dipper," Wilt Chamberlain, in his youth had no intention of playing basketball but was so tall the game discovered him. Many now regard Chamberlain as the greatest center in the history of the game, even though he was one of the poorest shooters ever from the free throw line. Chamberlain began his career with the Harlem Globetrotters and went on to play for three professional teams and won the NBA championships twice.

Michael Jordan (February 17, 1963–)   Although Michael Jordan is now retired from playing professional basketball, he is regarded by many as the best basketball player in the history of the game. Jordan played thirteen seasons for the Chicago Bulls and two seasons with the Washington Wizards. He won six NBA Championships (1991–1993 and 1996–1998) and was league MVP five times (1988, 1991, 1992, 1996, and 1998).

"Big Daddy" Eugene Lipscomb (August 9, 1931–May 10, 1963)   When he couldn't remember names, Lipscomb called people "little daddy" and so he became known as "Big Daddy." He had a difficult childhood and when he was eleven, Lipscomb's mother was murdered on her way to work. A 6-foot 6-inch, 284-pound defensive tackle, Lipscomb was larger than life. He was so dominant and his ability so legendary, that Lipscomb was able to joke with a grain of truth, "I just wrap my arms around the whole backfield and peel 'em one by one until I get to the ball carrier. Him I keep."

Lipscomb was also a professional wrestler where he portrayed heroes rather than the villains, which is what he seemed to running backs on the football field. But in both sports he is remembered for his good nature. Lipscomb died at thirty-one due to an overdose of heroine.

Joe Louis (May 13, 1914–April 12, 1981)   Joe Louis, The Brown Bomber, was heavy weight champion of the world from 1937 to 1949, the longest reign of all time. He fought in twenty-seven heavyweight championship fights, a record which still stands, and the prestige and wealth he earned were a symbol of hope to Blacks during the Great Depression. Louis remained a messenger of goodwill throughout his life.

His best remembered fight was a historical bout with Max Schmeling, a German national boxing hero prior to World War Two. On their first meeting, Schmeling was victorious and Nazi officials declared the fight proof of "Aryan superiority." Pound for pound the greatest boxer who ever lived, Sugar Ray Leonard years later reminisced that he had been devastated by Louis's loss, a feeling shared by many Americans. However, Louis and Schmeling met in a rematch that lasted all of two minutes and four seconds, with Louis the winner. Louis's redemptive victory was portrayed as justification of American democracy.

During the war, Louis enlisted in the segregated army. Asked how he felt about that considering his celebrity status, Louis replied, "Lots of things wrong with America, but Hitler ain't going to fix them."

Following the war, Louis was hounded for millions of dollars in unpaid taxes on prize winnings, and had to put off retirement and pride and enter the ring far past his prime in order to pay off the debt. In the mid-1960s, Louis was finally free of debt, but nothing remained of his past fortune. He did, however, have millions of fans, and a wealth of friends and supporters until the end of his life.

Jessie Owens (September 12, 1913–March 31, 1980) Born James Cleveland Owens he became Jesse when "J.C" was misheard by a schoolteacher. Raised in a poor Cleveland ghetto, Owens had the benefit of excellent coaching in high school and then at Ohio State University, where he had great success in track and field. But his moment of greatest recognition came in the 1936 Summer Olympics in Berlin, where he achieved international acclaim by winning four gold medals: in the 100m sprint, the long jump, the 200m sprint, and the 4 x 100m relay, an Olympic feat unequaled until Carl Lewis in 1984.

Augmenting the drama of his accomplishment, Owens's Olympic masterpiece created a controversy as to whether or not Hitler, presiding over the games, had refused to shake his hand. Owens refused to allow a politicization of the event when he pointed out that President Roosevelt hadn't recognized his accomplishment either, by telegram or otherwise.

After the Olympics, Jesse returned to the promise of lucrative contracts in the States, but the promises fell through and Owens was bankrupt and had to rebuild his career. However, Owens did remake himself and became "a goodwill ambassador" to high-profile American companies and traveled the world, at last given due for his Olympic accomplishments.

Satchel Paige (July 7, 1905–June 8, 1982) Someone once said he looked like a satchel tree, a comic description of what Leroy Robert Paige looked like when he was a young man working as a porter carrying "satchels." From then on Leroy Robert was called "Satchel" Paige. Often regarded as the greatest pitcher of his time, Satchel was "Jim Crowed" in the Negro Leagues from 1926 through 1948, so he played much of his career out of the mainstream spotlight. His exploits on the mound are legendary, such as once pitching from a rocking chair. Like Yogi Berra, he has good natured and humorous quotes on every subject from how to eat to how to stay young: "We get old when we stop playin." According to his fellow athletes and the pundits, he had no muscular development at all but he threw like a whip. He had a repertoire of pitches, like the blooper, the looper, the whipsey dipsey doo, and the bee ball, and he threw these pitches concealed behind his foot which he kicked up in front of him in a unique delivery.

In 1948, at forty-two years of age he signed with the Cleveland Indians, and was an instant celebrity. In his first year with the Indians, he helped them reach the World Series and was the first African American to pitch in the World Series, which the Indians won, and Satchel was awarded rookie of the year somewhat discrediting his years of fame in the Negro Leagues. Satchel played until 1959, when he became the oldest man to pitch in a major-league game. He was inducted into the Hall of Fame and in his speech Satchel reminisced about his former teammates and the players that baseball had so long kept from view in the Negro Leagues.

Paul Robeson (April 9, 1898–January 23, 1976) His father an escaped slave from a Carolina plantation and his mother from a distinguished Philadelphia family, Paul Robeson grew up in Princeton, New Jersey, and became the epitome of a Renaissance man. He was a talented athlete, an actor, and a singer. He was fluent in several languages, an author, and a political activist who championed civil rights. At Rutgers University he lettered in football, baseball, basketball, and track and field, and was the class valedictorian. Living in Harlem, New York City, Robeson attended Columbia University Law School, sang at the Cotton Club, acted in plays, and supported his family playing professional football. He received a law degree from Columbia, had a short career in law, but his deep voice and love of the stage and public speaking launched him on an acting career in stage and film. Robeson spoke out against segregation and lynching, and in the 1940s his political commitments became foremost in his life. His activism drew the attention of Senator Joseph McCarthy. Robeson's passport was revoked and his acting career curtailed and he disappeared from public life until his death in 1976. Robeson's funeral was attended by thousands admiring and recognizing the gifted accomplishments of this man.

Jackie Robinson (January 31, 1919–October 24, 1972) Jack Roosevelt "Jackie" Robinson broke the "color lines" in 1948 when he became the first African American to play in major-league baseball. Prior to his baseball career he was drafted to serve in World War II, but when he refused to give up his seat on a segregated military bus, he was court-martialed. He took the same defiance for civil injustice into his baseball career and wherever he went. On the field, Robinson was a fierce competitor and athletes and spectators alike were awed at displays of his athletic ability. All the while Robinson remained undeterred as pitches were thrown at him and he was taunted and ridiculed by opposing players for being Black, but which pushed him on and only further motivated, and

united his fans and teammates with his cause. A hero and a role model for Blacks for his courage and his will to play the game on his own terms, his example went far beyond baseball, where Robinson was a World Series champion and inducted into the Hall of Fame.

Robinson fought for civil rights in more places than on the baseball field. He denounced Jim Crow segregation, and when he traveled refused separate eating and sleeping arrangements in restaurants and hotels, and many were forced to change their policies on his account. Robinson was an outspoken advocate of Martin Luther King, Jr., and Malcolm X and he served on the board of the NAACP until 1967.

Sugar Ray Robinson (May 3, 1921–April 12, 1989) Born Walker Smith, Jr., someone once remarked that Robinson's fluid ability was "sweet as sugar," and so he became Sugar Ray. From Harlem, New York City, Robinson became "pound for pound" the greatest boxer who ever lived. Like his boyhood idol Joe Louis, Robinson too was chased by the IRS for tax evasion, and even though Sugar Ray had retired from boxing for a show business career, he was forced to come out of his retirement to fight younger opponents to satisfy his debts to the IRS. Robinson fought well into his forties, and his fame faded. He died in 1989, poor and his legacy obscured, but resurrected in recent years.

WRITERS AND POETS

James Baldwin (August 6, 1924–November 30, 1987) Baldwin was a gifted novelist, playwright, poet, essayist, and civil rights activist. Most of his work deals with racial and sexual issues in the mid-twentieth century United States. However, his novels are notable for the personal way in which they explore questions of identity as well as for the way in which they deal with the pressures related to being Black and homosexual. He brought these issues to the forefront of his novels before the social, cultural, and political equality was discussed in the mainstream.

Gwendolyn Brooks (June 7, 1917–December 3, 2000)   She gave expression to the truth that Black is beautiful. A child of the lost generation and the Harlem Renaissance, she became a superstar among authors. She wrote about being Black and a woman with unparalleled craftsman in poetry. Brooks was the first Black to win a Pulitzer Prize in 1950. She wrote about urban Blacks who encountered racism.

Sterling Allen Brown (May 1, 1901–January 13, 1989)   Brown was an African-American professor, author of works on folklore, poetry, and literary criticism, and a poet. He was interested chiefly in Black culture of the southern United States. Although his poetry was largely neglected during his lifetime, he had an uncanny ability to write about the everyday folk.

Brown spent most of his life as an English professor at Howard University, where he taught courses ranging from Shakespeare to World Literature and influencing a new generation of students—Amiri Baraka and Gwendolyn Brooks are his two most famous.

Rita Dove (August 28, 1952–)   She is an American poet and author and the second African-American poet to win the Pulitzer Prize (after Gwendolyn Brooks in 1950). From 1993 to 1995, she served as the second Black and the youngest Poet Laureate of the United States and Poetry Consultant to the Library of Congress.

She published six poetry collections, among them *Thomas and Buelah,* which was awarded the Pulitzer Prize in 1987. She is also the author of the novel *Through the Ivory Gate* and the drama

The Darker Face of the Earth, which premiered at the Oregon Shakespeare Festival in 1996 and was subsequently produced at the Kennedy Center in Washington, D.C., and other theaters. Her song cycle *Seven for Luck,* with music by John Williams, was first performed with the Boston Symphony Orchestra at Tanglewood in 1998.

Paul Lawrence Dunbar (June 27, 1872–February 9, 1906)   One of the first Black poets to attain national and international recognition for his 1896 "Lyrics of a Lowly Life," a poem in the collection *Ode to Ethiopia.*

Ralph Walden Ellison (March 1, 1914–April 16, 1994)   Ellison's father named him after writer Ralph Waldo Emerson because he had great hopes for his future. Ellison's original art of choice was jazz. He started writing at the suggestion of Langston Hughes and Richard Wright. Once Ellison started, he wrote essays, reviews, and short stories for various periodicals. He also became the editor of the *Negro Quarterly.*

In 1952, Ellison wrote his first novel, *Invisible Man,* about an alienated and isolated Black man living in a racially repressed America. The book's success made him one of the most famous and important writers of his time. For the next forty years he would work on his next novel, but he died before it was completed.

Harlem Renaissance (1920)   During the roaring twenties, in speakeasies during prohibition, Blacks were able to make Harlem their own part of New York City. Literature, art, music, and social commentary flourished. American descendents of European cultures (read White America) were exposed to the thoughts, dreams, and creativity of Blacks.

Langston Hughes (February 1, 1902–May 22, 1967)   One of the most versatile and prolific writers of the Harlem Renaissance period, penning poetry, novels, plays, short stories, and columns. He promoted the beauty and heritage of Blacks in America and spoke on social, economic, and political justice issues.

Zora Neal Hurston (January 7, 1891–January 28, 1960)   Hurston is an anthropologist, novelist, folklorist, and authority on Black culture. During the Harlem Renaissance she is best known for penning the 1937 novel *Their Eyes Were Watching God.* The book was inspired by Eatonville, Florida, the first all-Black town to be incorporated in the United States.

James Weldon Johnson (June 17, 1871–June 26, 1938)   This author, teacher, lawyer, critic, politician, poet, and songwriter wrote the Black national anthem, "Lift Every Voice and Sing."

Yusef Komunyakaa (April 29, 1947–)   Born James Willie Brown, Jr., this poet and educator writes about the African-American experience in the South before the civil rights movement and his experiences as a soldier during the Vietnam War. He has won several awards including the 1994 Pulitzer Prize for Poetry.

Claude McKay (September 15, 1889–May 22, 1948)   Although born in Jamaica, McKay was involved in the Harlem Renaissance and wrote three novels: *Home to Harlem* (1928), a best-seller which won the Harmon Gold Award for Literature, *Banjo* (1929), and *Banana Bottom* (1933). He also wrote a collection of short stories, *Gingertown* (1932) and two autobiographical books, *A Long Way from Home* (1937), and *Harlem: Negro Metropolis* (1940). His book of poetry, *Harlem Shadows* (1922) was among the first books published during the Harlem Renaissance. His book of collected poems, *Selected Poems* (1953), was published after his death.

Toni Morrison (February 18, 1831–)   Toni Morrison, born Chloe Anthony Wofford, has written novels that illuminate the experiences and roles of Black women in a racist and male-dominated society. Entwined into her stories of complex and multilayered narratives is a detailed understanding of the African-American culture. Among her best known novels are *The Bluest Eye, Song of Solomon, Tar Baby*, and *Beloved.*

Beyond receiving great acclaim Mrs. Morrison has won many awards including the Pulitzer Prize for Fiction for *Beloved* and the Nobel Prize for Literature, the first for a Black woman.

Jean Toomer (December 26, 1894–March 30, 1967)   Born Nathan Pinchback Toomer, this writer and philosopher wrote many articles, poems, short stories, and narratives during his career. His novel, *Cane*, was published in 1923 and is considered the first book to usher in the Harlem Renaissance in literature.

Alice Walker (February 9, 1944–)   A self-declared feminist and womanist—the latter a term she herself coined to make special distinction for the experiences of women of color—Walker is a talent author. She has written at length on issues of race and gender, and is most famous for the critically acclaimed novel *The Color Purple,* for which she won the Pulitzer Prize for Fiction.

Margaret Walker (July 6, 1915–November 30, 1998)   Although her full name is Dr. Margaret Abigail Walker Alexander, this prize-winning poet wrote as Margaret Walker. Her literature generally contained African-American themes.

Among her more popular works were her poem "For My People," which won the Yale Series of Younger Poets Competition, and her 1966 novel *Jubilee,* which received critical acclaim. In 1988, she sued Alex Haley, claiming his novel *Roots: The Saga of an American Family* had violated *Jubilee*'s copyright. The case was dismissed. Margaret Walker was the first African-American woman to receive a Ph.D.

Phillis Wheatley (1753–December 5, 1784) The first published African-American poet whose writings helped create the genre of African-American literature. She was born in Gambia, Africa, and became a slave at age seven. Purchased by the Boston Wheatley family, they taught her to read and write, and helped encouraged her poetry.

The 1773 publication of Wheatley's *Poems on Various Subjects, Religious and Moral*, brought her fame, with dignitaries such as George Washington praising her work. Wheatley also toured England and was praised in a poem by fellow African-American poet Jupiter Hammon. Wheatley was emancipated by her owners after her poetic success, but stayed with the Wheatley family until the death of her former master and the breakup of his family. She died in poverty in 1784 while working on a second book of poetry, which has been lost.

Walt Whitman (May 31, 1819–March 26, 1892) An American poet, essayist, journalist, and humanist, he was a part of the transition between Transcendentalism and realism, incorporating both views in his works. Whitman is among the most influential poets in the American canon, often called the father of free verse. His work was very controversial in its time, particularly his poetry collection *Leaves of Grass,* which was described as obscene for its overt sexuality. Whitman was concerned with politics throughout his life. He supported the Wilmot Proviso and opposed the extension of slavery generally, but did not believe in the abolitionist movement.

Richard Wright (September 4, 1908–November 28, 1960) Wright wrote powerful, sometimes controversial, novels, short stories, and nonfiction that helped redefine discussions of race relations in America. The success of *Uncle Tom's Children* in 1938 and *Native Son* in 1940 propelled Wright to international fame.

note from the author

The historical images in this book are the never-before-seen original works of Romare Bearden, one of this country's greatest draftsmen. The audacity to present twenty images created by use of a ball-point pen and saturated marker on porous paper where any indecision would be immediately destructive, is the work of a true master in complete control of his discipline.

—Russell Goings

about the author

Russell L. Goings was born at the height of the Depression in Stamford, Connecticut, on July 5, 1932.

His school in Stamford categorized him as dyslexic and exiled him to a class of slow learners. By the time he reached high school, it was becoming increasingly apparent that he had a keen mind. He was invited to Princeton for a college visit. Instead of Princeton, Goings enlisted in the U.S. Air Force, which had no difficulty recognizing his abilities. Placing near the top of incoming recruits in terms of intelligence and mental agility, he was dispatched to an elite school in Japan and then assigned to the U.S. Strategic Air Command to train pilots in escape and evasion. After leaving the service in 1955, Goings enrolled in Xavier University in Cincinnati, Ohio. He completed his undergraduate degree in two years, finishing in the top 10 percent of his class, and then spent the next two years on a graduate scholarship working towards a master's degree in economics. Six hours short of completing his master's, his life took another turn when he was offered a contract as a professional football player, at first in Canada and then with the Buffalo Bills.

When Goings's football career ended after a series of injuries, he turned to Wall Street. Shearson Hammill asked him to come on board as the first Afro-American branch manager of a New York Stock Exchange firm. He opened an office on 125th Street, in Harlem. On October 1, 1971, he managed to buy out Shearson's interest in the brokerage and establish his own company, First Harlem Securities. That month, First Harlem became the first fully operational Afro-American brokerage to have its own seat on the New York Stock Exchange. He helped found and became the first Afro-American chairman of the Studio Museum in Harlem, and he also helped found and became the first chairman of *Essence* magazine.

Eventually losing interest in the financial struggles on Wall Street, Goings turned completely to art. He was a close friend of the celebrated Afro-American painter and collagist Romare Bearden. When Bearden developed cancer, during Goings's daily visits, as a distraction from the pain, Bearden insisted that Goings make up stories. The practice hooked Goings on writing. He then enrolled in the writing program at Fairfield University and later at the 92nd Street Y.

Over a lifetime, seventy-six-year-old Goings has been featured in *The New York Times, Newsweek, Black Enterprise,* as well as in other esteemed publications. This Renaissance man has been inducted into the Wall Street Hall of Fame, received literary awards for fiction and poetry from Fairfield University, and he has also received the highest award of Alpha Sigma Nu for Lifetime Achievement.

art index

The art featured in this book is from Mr. Russell L. Goings's private collection.

c. 1986